CONTENTS

FOREWORD

Hi! I'm Rashida, Kidada's younger sister. From a very early age, I could tell that Kidada struggled with learning and school. My parents tried their best to find her the right fit, but it never quite worked. But when it came to playtime, she was a magician. She knew how to turn closets into spaceships, shoes into sports cars, and dolls into friends. She would draw everybody, me and all my friends, into a different world. My sister is an incredibly unique human: she's imaginative, she challenges the system, she thinks and feels deeply. You could say Kidada marches to the beat of her own drum, and she has come to champion her uniqueness as her best quality. This amazing, interactive book is the result of her dedication to nurturing her inner life, and it's her way of sharing all the great tools she has discovered along the way. It presents loads of activities and insights that could only come from someone who has learned the value of her true self, her spirit, and her complexities.

My first thought after reading *School of Awake*: I really wish I'd had this book much earlier in my life! It would have helped me with self-acceptance. Being a successful person is about building a character that combines all the best parts of who we are, in a way that unites our minds and our hearts. Hopefully, *School of Awake* will help you do that and will give you the life skills you'll need to cope with any challenges that come up in your life, internally and externally. And it's a ton of fun, full of adventure, wisdom, and power! You'll want to return to *School of Awake* again and again, and you'll always discover something new. Enjoy!!   — *Rashida Jones*

WELCOME TO SCHOOL OF AWAKE!

What if you could go to a school that taught you the secrets of what we know on the inside but rarely talk about, the universal laws that have guided visionaries for centuries? A school that taught you how to move through the world with confidence and ease, and gave you tools to develop all the jewels that lived inside your heart so that you could become the very best version of yourself? That's the question I used to think about when I was a little girl. Although I'm a product designer by day, I have always been and always will be a full-time student of my inner self.

I struggled my way through 11 schools, both private and public, and I was held back twice and kicked out of 8 schools. These schools were based on traditional education and focused on general subjects. While these subjects are crucial, I craved a different type of education about who I was inside and how to navigate my emotional and spiritual world. I wanted to be in the classroom of the heart and learn about the potential I held as a young girl. Life became my teacher.

All the things we know deep down inside our hearts in our quiet moments are the things I felt compelled to explore. How are we all connected? How do I build close relationships? What does it mean to have good qualities? How do I believe in my dreams? I wanted to become the best person I could be and learn all about the authentic power I held inside. When we are young, our hearts carry a certain magic of knowing and embracing our dreams, a magic we sometimes forget. When I was 9 years old I knew that one day I had to write a book that would be helpful for girls. It was something I just knew I would do.

Through all my young years of trials and tribulations, amazing joys, and devastating losses, my heart's guidance was always there for me, reminding me of what mattered most. My inspiration was to create a classroom called School of Awake™, a classroom that teaches everything I have learned along the way. This book is a gift to my younger self — and to you — full of fun, interactive ways to not only get to know yourself but also learn to love who you are and discover the potential of who you can become.

School of Awake (S.O.A.) is for the goddess that lives within every girl in the process of becoming a woman and every woman who is honoring her inner girl. May we continue to learn to love ourselves. May we never forget our inner power as compassionate, loving creators of this world.

Love,
Kidada

Hey, Star Babies!

Welcome! I'm so happy this book is in your hands. "Why?" you might ask. Because this book is for the new school of dreamers, light beings, and game changers who are ready to learn about the true power and love that we all hold inside our hearts. It's time to access the light and excellence that we are all capable of. Time to be champions of goodness.

This book is full of truths, things you already know and feel deep down in your heart but might need to be reminded of. You are a sorceress, a goddess, a star child! A mini universe! You are like a garden ready to bloom with beautiful, tremendous potential. Wouldn't it be amazing to have some tools to help you become your supreme self and to be able to return to that space again and again, especially when the going gets tough? Let's learn how to connect to the timelessness that lives within us all. Let's celebrate our girlhood and build our inner goddess energy.

SOUL-SOOTHING TOOL KIT

We're going to make a tool kit out of a shoe box. This will not be just any old shoe box. This shoe box is going to hold all the tools you need to be your supreme self.

As you read the book and complete the activities, you are going to fill this box with art, treasures, and other bits of goodness. By the end of the book you will have a treasure chest of special things that you can go to whenever you need a piece of comfort or a source of strength. Whenever you need to dream, wish, imagine, or just get through a situation, your tool kit will be waiting and ready to go! Let's do this!

NOTE ON SUPPLIES

School of Awake encourages affordable creativity! We have created each of the activities in this book for less than $5.00 by shopping at our local dollar and discount stores. We also encourage you to repurpose items from your home whenever possible for your crafts. And you may wish to buy an inexpensive notebook or journal to keep in your tool kit for jotting down notes or responding to the fun questions and quizzes called "S.O.A. Moments."

WE ARE ALL STARDUST

CHAPTER ONE

THE CHEMICAL ELEMENTS THAT MAKE UP OUR BODIES

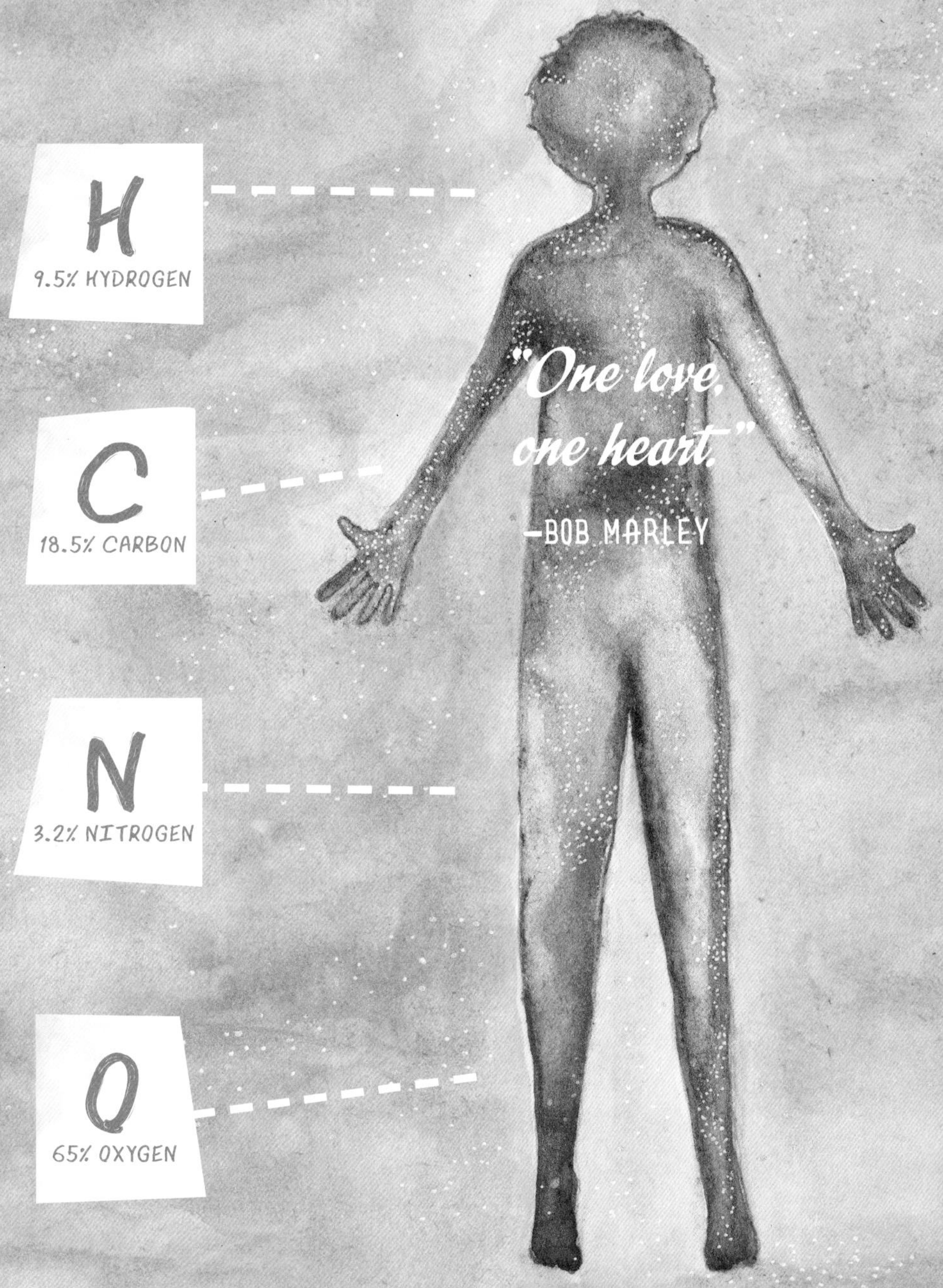

H
9.5% HYDROGEN

C
18.5% CARBON

N
3.2% NITROGEN

O
65% OXYGEN

"One love, one heart."
—BOB MARLEY

Did you know that you are made of the same material as stars? Astrophysicists, including the brilliant Neil deGrasse Tyson, have taught us that the same reactions that create the dazzling light in stars created life on planet Earth. The molecules and atoms in our bodies contain the same chemicals that stars are made of. WE ARE ALL STARDUST. All animals, nature, and everything we can see with our human eyes and beyond have a connection through molecules.

> *"We are all connected — to each other, biologically;*
> *to the earth, chemically; to the rest of*
> *the universe, atomically."*
> —NEIL DEGRASSE TYSON

Breaking it down to a micro level, the main ingredient everything in the known universe shares is carbon. Carbon shooting into the galaxy created our stars and planets, merging with clouds that collapsed and eventually created humans. Another element we share is hydrogen. We all have hydrogen in us! Hydrogen, the lightest and simplest element, is also a main ingredient of the visible universe. We also carry oxygen and nitrogen, and these 4 elements combine to make up a human body as well as everything in our universe. All the stars that have exploded over time have released these ingredients into the cosmos. Generation after generation, stars explode and help to create us and the world we experience. We are part of the universe, and the universe is part of us.

Even the people that get on my nerves... We are all one?

Wowzers!

Yup... We all come from the same source

WHEN WE THINK ABOUT IT THAT WAY, HOW CAN WE NOT LOVE EACH OTHER?

FACT

Astronomers believe that many of the elements in the human body were formed by supernovas. Supernovas occur when stars exhaust their fuel at the end of their life cycles and then explode, spewing stardust throughout the cosmos. In 2008, astrophysicist Alicia Soderberg of Princeton University and several of her colleagues became the first human beings to witness and record a supernova as it actually happened.

S.O.A. MOMENT

Thoughts are seeds, and wishes are powerful! 11:11 is a magical time. Look at the digits that make up 11:11 — together they basically form 2 open doors. School of Awake believes this number creates a gateway to the heavens for wishes to come true. Whenever you see that it's 11:11 AM or PM, look up at the sky, close your eyes, and make a wish. You can make the same wish over and over or switch it up and make a new wish each time. School of Awake likes to make wishes for the world to be a better place so everyone benefits.

TIPS FOR MAKING A WISH

Wish for things that don't hurt anyone or harm anything. Keep your wish pure!

Don't worry about the *how?* of a wish coming true. Just stay focused on your wish.

Wish for things that benefit everyone, not just material objects.

Be excited and visualize your wish already being a reality.

Be grateful and thank the universe as if your wish has already come true.

Wishes are on their own schedule and come true at the right time. Don't rush a wish!

THERE IS A BIGGER PICTURE HERE

We have bodies, names, identities that make us feel separate from everyone and everything, when we really are not separate. Imagine the ocean and how vast it is. It is enormous! Now imagine millions and trillions of tiny water drops coming together to make this huge ocean. That's us. We are smaller pieces of a massive, moving source, the same source that lives within each of us. When we look up into the magical night sky or at the clouds during the day, we can remember that everything in this world is all part of the same oneness. No matter what our differences appear to be, we are all connected.

There are over a hundred billion galaxies in this universe, beyond anything our human minds can even comprehend. New galaxies are being formed all the time. All this magic is happening on its own, not because a human is making it happen but because there is a force greater than us humans. A force that knows no limits and is boundless. That force lives in every element and molecule in all galaxies and universes, and it lives within all of us. We are all connected to a higher intelligence that keeps every living being on this earth alive.

WOW. I AM POWERFUL.

S.O.A. MOMENT — Cosmic Connection

FILL IN THE BLANKS:

1. Knowing that I'm made up of stardust makes me feel _____.

2. At night when I look at the stars I feel _____.

3. The word *oneness* reminds me that I'm _____.

4. I feel my greatest contribution to this planet will be _____.

5. If I could make one wish for the whole world it would be _____.

6. The thing I appreciate most about the universe is _____.

7. If I were a constellation, my name would be _____.

8. I feel most connected to the universe when _____.

FACT:

The groupings of stars in the sky have been studied from earliest times, and these constellations have been named based on the shapes that would be formed by drawing lines connecting the stars. You've probably picked out the Big Dipper, for example. What other shapes do you see?

ANSWER THIS:

Which of these are real constellation names and which aren't?

a. Draco
b. Orion
c. Cassiopeia
d. Phoenix
e. Pegasus
f. Scorpius

ANSWER: All of these are the names of real constellations! Look them up to discover what shapes they represent.

When we can feel the connection we all have in the world, we can understand that we are part of something bigger. We each have tremendous power inside, just like the power of the stars. We realize how special it is to be alive, and we really treasure our lives. Knowing that we are all connected gives us a responsibility to be a great version of ourselves and consider how we affect everything around us. What we do touches everything.

What we do touches everything.

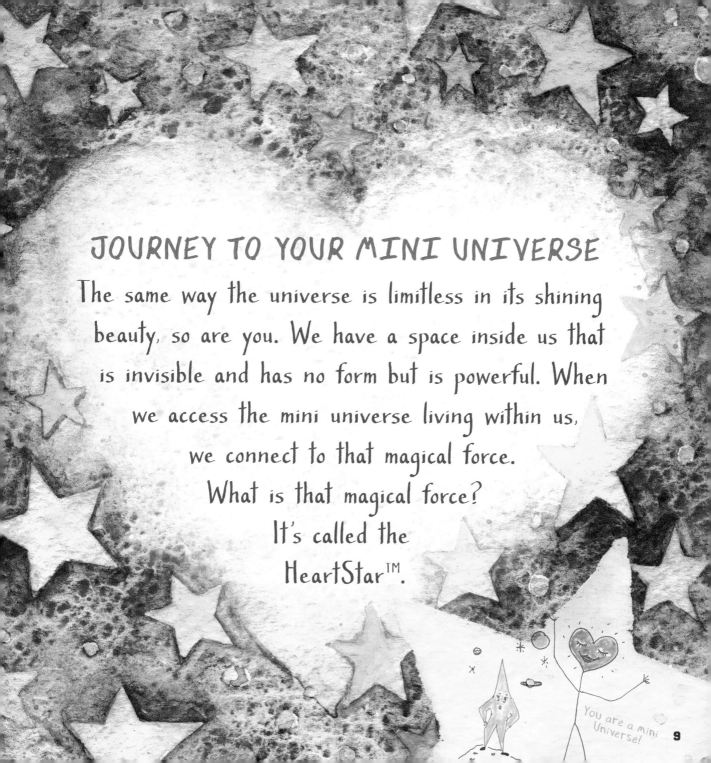

JOURNEY TO YOUR MINI UNIVERSE

The same way the universe is limitless in its shining beauty, so are you. We have a space inside us that is invisible and has no form but is powerful. When we access the mini universe living within us, we connect to that magical force.
What is that magical force?
It's called the
HeartStar™.

You are a mini Universe!

The HeartStar

Our HeartStar is something that is invisible and can only be felt. It feels like knowing, it feels like love, it feels like home. We know when we are connected to our HeartStar because we feel joyful and happy. We make good choices and are kind and loving to ourselves and other people. When we are not connected to our HeartStar, something feels off. We feel closed, moody, and fearful, and sometimes we're unkind.

Have you ever known something deep down inside, but your mind keeps telling you other things, and you ignore the tiny voice you keep hearing and feeling inside, only to later come around to realizing the tiny voice inside was right all along? That's the space we are talking about.

This HeartStar will never steer you wrong or leave you. Your HeartStar has been with you since you were born and loves you more than anyone in the world. It is always available, whenever you need counsel. Consider your HeartStar your built-in GPS that wants to guide you to the best version of yourself. It's your bestie. When we get quiet and breathe, our HeartStar is waiting to give us the answers we need.

HORIZON OF HAPPINESS

LAKE OF LOVE

OCEAN OF KNOWING

BEACH OF KINDNESS

DUNES OF DEEP BREATHING

N

W HOME E

S

CAMP CALM

GARDEN OF GOODNESS

RIVER OF TRUTH

BESTIE BAY

INNER VOICE ISLAND

How do we get there? Well, first we learn to breathe. When we pay attention to how we are breathing, we are brought back to our mini universe, where our HeartStar lives. Sometimes all our thinking gets in the way and makes it easy to forget what we hold inside our hearts. Breathing guides us back to that inner space and also reminds us that we are always connected to that massive source. Think of breathing as the highway back to your mini universe where the HeartStar is waiting.

SO YOU'RE TELLING ME THIS BECAUSE...?

You have a guidance system in your body that's called your HeartStar. Whenever you feel lost or confused or need to make big decisions in your life, or even if you just feel cranky, check in with your HeartStar and breathe. Your HeartStar is joyful and loving by nature and will help you stay connected to your truth.

SHORTCUTS TO THE HEARTSTAR

- Cuddle with your pet
- Laugh with a friend
- Go be in nature
- Dance and sing to your favorite song
- Do what you love to do
- Move your body
- Help someone who needs you
- Just cry and let it out
- Share your true feelings
- Punch your pillow

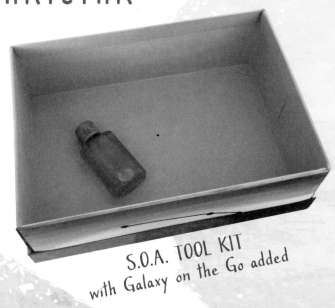

S.O.A. TOOL KIT
with Galaxy on the Go added

ACTIVITY ⚠ ALERT

GALAXY ON THE GO!

Let's make a mini universe!
A pocket-size reminder of the wonder
that lives within us all.
🩵⭐🩵

Step 1: Squeeze 10 pinches of glitter into your empty bottle.

Step 2: Fill the bottle with water.

Step 3: Add 2 or 3 drops of food coloring.

Step 4: Put the top back on, and shake it all up.

 1.   2.   3.   4.

Jupiter is the planet of wishes!!! Traditionally, in astrology, it represents expansion, blessings, and good fortune. Jupiter is 365,000,000 miles from Earth. Write this number somewhere on your mini universe. Whenever you need a reminder of your inner shine and want to make a wish, sit quietly with your Galaxy on the Go, shake it up, close your eyes & send your wish out to Jupiter.*

*You can also shake your mini universe at 11:11 AM or PM to activate your wish.

THE BRIDGE TO YOUR INNER WORLD: BREATHING

CHAPTER TWO

There is so much power in an inhale and an exhale. Who knew that something that comes so naturally for us could be the most precious gift we are given in this lifetime? Not only does breathing keep us alive and feed our brains and bodies with oxygen, but breathing connects us to a truth inside: the space of love. Breathing is the secret bridge from the world outside us to the magical world inside us. Breathing reminds us we are here and connected to our inner (and outer) worlds. When we bring our focus to our breathing, we are connecting to our life force. For that reason, we'll add it to our School of Awake tool kit!

FACT By breathing slowly and deeply, you can activate your parasympathetic nervous system, and this is the part of your body that can help reverse and calm your strong reaction to stress. Deep, slow breathing can stimulate the vagus nerve, the main nerve in the parasympathetic nervous system. Then your heart rate will slow down and your body and mind will become more calm.

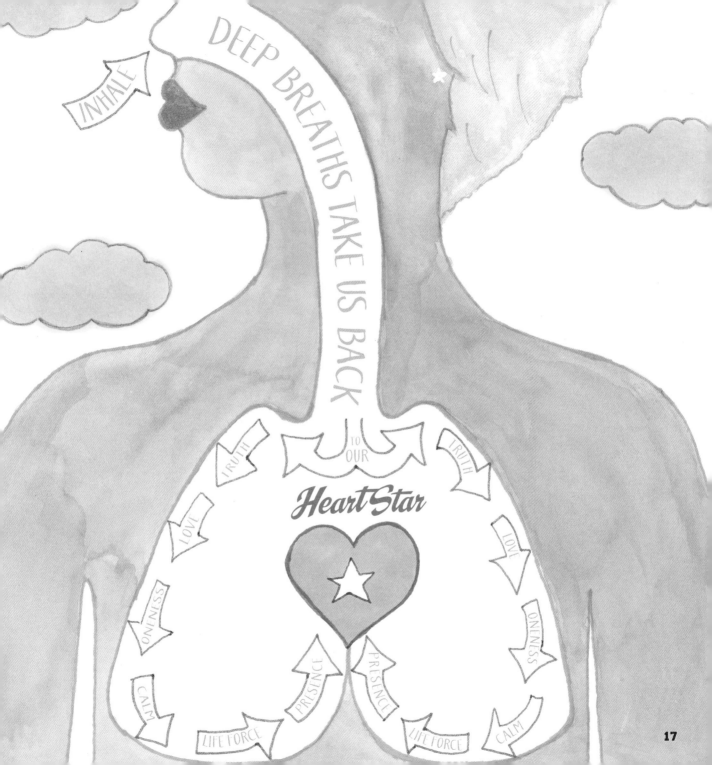

17

We can learn a lot about how we are feeling by the way we breathe. When we feel happy, our breathing flows easily and deeply. When we feel sad or angry or stressed, our breathing gets shorter and tighter.

It's really easy to forget you're actually breathing because it comes naturally and happens without your thinking about it. Focused breathing is just remembering that you are breathing, and then making an effort to pay attention to how your breath actually feels in your body. Time slows down when we remember to breathe.

Breathing in deeply and slowly is healing and uplifting. Try it now: breathe slowly through your nose as you count to 5, and exhale the same way. School of Awake calls this *conscious breathing*. Breathing consciously throughout the day will be the best gift you can give yourself. Taking the time to breathe consciously will always connect you back to your HeartStar.

KEY MOMENTS FOR CONSCIOUS BREATHING

- When you are searching for the right thing to say, take a deep breath first.
- Always take a few deep breaths before making big decisions.
- Breathe before you respond to someone who is aggravating you.
- Breathe before you eat to express gratitude, help with your digestion, and enjoy your meal.
- Breathe when you feel nervous or scared!
- Take long, deep breaths to fall asleep quickly.

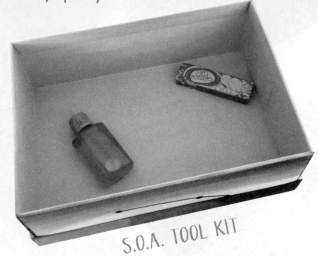

S.O.A. TOOL KIT

ACTIVITY ⚠ ALERT
BUBBLE GUM *Chill*

BUBBLE GUM CHILL NOTE

By counting and blowing, you can measure whether you're breathing in enough air for the bubble, and if not, you'll learn quickly how to fill your lungs and the gum with air!

Chew and keep repeating your breathing technique for 1 minute with your eyes closed. Before you know it, you will be so chill!

INHALE . . . .

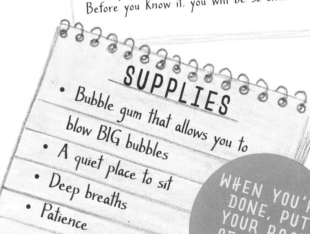

Step 1: Chew gum past the point of full flavor.

Step 2: Close your eyes, and take a deep breath in for 5 counts. 1 . . . 2 . . . 3 . . . 4 . . . 5

Step 3: Blow out very slowly, and as you do, start to blow a bubble.

Step 4: Bigger . . .

Step 5: Bigger . . .

Step 6: Let it pop.

Step 7: Repeat steps 2 through 6 for 1 minute.

EXHALE . . . .

SUPPLIES

- Bubble gum that allows you to blow BIG bubbles
- A quiet place to sit
- Deep breaths
- Patience

WHEN YOU'RE DONE, PUT YOUR PACK OF GUM IN YOUR TOOL KIT!

Studies have shown that breathing practices can reduce the symptoms, such as racing heart or sluggishness, often associated with anxiety, depression, attention deficit disorder, and insomnia.

GORILLA BREATHING EXERCISE

Have you ever seen gorillas pound on their chests and make noise? Gorillas are really shy by nature, and the act of pounding on their chests and letting out air to make noise actually gives them courage. It makes them feel brave. So School of Awake developed the gorilla breathing exercise to use anytime we need a bit of courage! Let's try it:

LET IT RIP

Write down something that makes you scared or nervous, then stand firmly with your feet hip-width apart and take 5 to 10 slow, deep breaths in and out. After a deep inhale, exhale while letting out the sound "ahhhhhhhhh," and lightly beat your chest (not too hard and not too loud). Your voice should be shaky on the way out. Do this a few times in a row, getting louder if it feels good to get louder.

Now how do you feel? Do you feel more courageous? You can do this every morning or whenever you're having a hard time expressing yourself. It will help you find your words and give you an extra boost of confidence.

I'm feeling it!

MINDFULNESS

Another tool we have — free and available anytime we need it — is something called *mindfulness*. What does being mindful mean? Well, now that we've experienced the power of conscious breathing, we are in the perfect space to begin learning mindfulness.

Being mindful is almost like being a witness to your thoughts and your actions. You become the watcher of your own behavior, floating above it all like a bird. You are breathing and taking in all the things about the present moment, not reacting or taking everything too seriously, but simply experiencing it. You're tapping into the quiet underneath everything. What does the room you are in look like? What do you smell? What do you hear? Focusing on your surroundings keeps you in a mindful state. Since Spider-Man has a sharp sense of sound and smell, let's call these the School of Awake *Spidey senses*. Mindfulness is tuning in to your sharp Spidey senses. You stop thinking about everything except what is right in front of you right now.

SNACK ALERT

MINI MINDFUL MOON POPS

FROM THE SCHOOL OF AWAKE KITCHEN

RECIPE

MIX AND MATCH FUN COMBOS!

INGREDIENTS

- 2 mini cookies or graham crackers
- 2 teaspoons peanut butter,* chocolate spread, cream cheese, or some other spread you love
- 1 tablespoon chocolate, vanilla, or strawberry ice cream

DIRECTIONS

Smear each cookie or graham cracker with the spread. Place them on a paper towel, on a plate, or in a resealable plastic bag, and put them in the freezer for about 20 minutes. Then take them out, add your tablespoon of ice cream on top of 1 of the cookies or graham crackers, and sandwich it with the other one.

*Caution: Not intended for those with peanut allergies.

Turn your lights low and pick 2 favorite songs to listen to. Eat your moon pop slowly, making it last for both songs with no distraction. Taste every bite. Be mindful of chewing, how it tastes, and your breathing. When we are aware of our senses we can become mindful.

MINI MINDFUL MOON POP COMBOS TO TRY

Try different flavor combinations for your mini mindful moon pops: graham crackers with strawberry ice cream, vanilla cookies with chocolate or vanilla ice cream, or peanut butter cookies with chocolate or vanilla ice cream.

TAKE 60 SECONDS TO...

- breathe and look around at your surroundings.
- notice the color of the room, the temperature, and all the details of what you see.
- feel the warmth in your hands and feet.
- blink your eyes and feel your eyelashes.
- wiggle your toes and move your shoulders.
- reMIND yourself you are in the present moment. Right now.

"Our true home is not in the past. Our true home is not in the future. Our true home is in the here and the now. Life is available only in the here and the now, and it is our true home."

—THICH NHAT HANH

When you are awake to your Spidey senses, suddenly everything will seem more alive, more vibrant. Colors will be brighter, noises louder, smells stronger.

Try it out. Start to look around to take notes on it all. What colors do you see? What texture is the wall? Can you feel your feet and hands?

It's like downloading a new operating system inside yourself. There is no past, there is no future, there is just now. You are now plugged into the present moment, and this is mindfulness.

SO YOU'RE TELLING ME THIS BECAUSE...?

Breathing and mindfulness are core tools that will serve you for your entire life. They will keep you grounded, present, and rooted in your personal power. When you feel like your mind is spinning or you're overthinking everything, all you have to do is remember to breathe and become mindful. Even if you don't like what's happening in this exact moment, becoming mindful will lift you above what's happening and help keep you calm. These tools will bring you into focus quickly and allow you to make choices from a place of alert awareness.

TRULY YOU

CHAPTER THREE

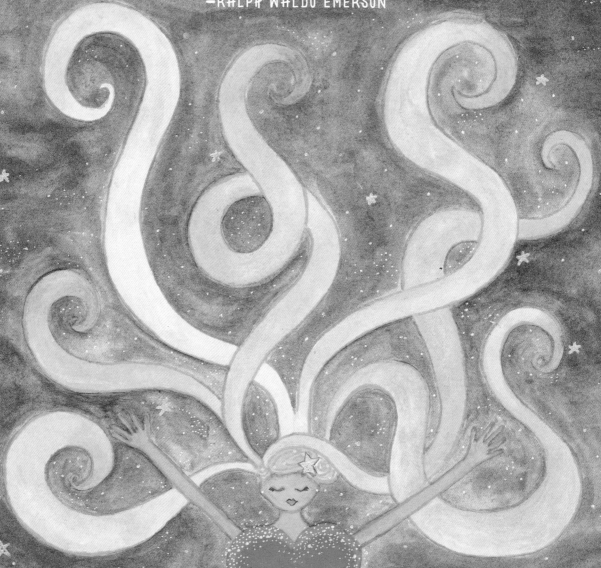

"To be yourself in a world that is constantly trying to make you something else is the greatest accomplishment."
—RALPH WALDO EMERSON

Wow, you're made of stardust and you're a witness with Spidey senses! You've connected to your HeartStar with breathing and mindfulness, but what about the outside? Are you who you think you are? You are more than what you see in the mirror. There is your outer identity (what you look like, where you live, your hobbies, and so on), and then there is who you are on the inside. We think we are our personalities and our likes and dislikes. But guess what? There is a much bigger being inside you. Believe it or not, these are separate things, even though we are taught to believe that we are who we THINK we are. Your outer identity sometimes gets in the way of your true self.

Thinking is good. Sometimes. Your mind is an amazing tool. It helps you with your tasks. It processes information and creates memories. It's the most incredible organ ever, but don't let your thinking take you over completely. Your heart and soul are the very things you connect to when you practice breathing and being mindful. When you're doing your favorite thing and really being yourself, you are in your zone and you are connected to your HeartStar, and that is bigger than your personality.

Does that make sense? Think of times in your life when time just stands still. Those moments when you are totally present and not thinking of anything except exactly what you are doing. It can happen while you're dancing, singing, painting, playing a sport, or doing anything that feels really good. When you're doing it, you look down at your clock and hours have passed and you have no clue how. That's the zone we are talking about. When you are in that space you are not overthinking. You are naturally more connected to your authentic self. That's your true self. That's where your knowing and goodness are always waiting for you. Learning to breathe and become mindful are gateways to get there, but the things that you really love doing are also gateways into your true nature.

Remember how you're made of stardust? That's the physical part. Inside, the heart and soul part, you are love. Underneath everything that you might doubt, feel, or think about yourself is pure love.

you shine

WHAT IS AUTHENTIC POWER?

Authentic power is knowing how to access the strongest parts of who you are from the inside and building an outer character that you love and respect. Being authentic takes a lot of courage and knowing who you are. A lot of people think that having money or having nice things or being popular and pretty is what makes them powerful or is necessary for them to be loved and respected. Our world puts a lot of importance on those things, but that's an illusion. That's not true power. Authenticity is knowing your value and self-worth separately from your physical traits or what others think is important, and not allowing anyone or anything to keep you from being that real part of yourself.

School of Awake calls the combination of your inner and outer self your *authentic self,* and when you can live as your authentic self, you live in your authentic power. True power is all yours, and it all starts with loving who you are from the inside out. The more you start to check in with your HeartStar and your breathing, the stronger that power becomes, because you are becoming more present and mindful. When you are present in the moment of now, you will begin to make choices in your life that come from a place of love. These choices will affect you and everyone around you. Authentic power is about building the parts of yourself that are rooted in goodness and cannot be taken away.

AUTHENTICITY IS KNOWING OUR VALUE AND SELF-WORTH

AND NOT ALLOWING ANYONE OR ANYTHING TO KEEP YOU FROM BEING THAT

YOURSELF THAT ARE ROOTED IN PRESENCE AND CANNOT BE TAKEN AWAY . . .

BE AUTHENTIC

NO MATTER WHAT

REAL PART OF YOURSELF • AUTHENTIC POWER IS ABOUT BUILDING THE PARTS OF

"All material things come and go, but who you are inside cannot be destroyed." —Kidada

You are the most important person you will ever meet. You will be spending the rest of your life with — guess who? — you! This relationship is the most critical relationship you will ever have. It is the one relationship that will affect every other relationship in your life. You can't love anyone else until you really love yourself. Self-love is about loving every single version of yourself, even when you think you are unlovable.

This journey of authenticity requires courage. Living up to an image of who you think you should be is not being authentic. Loving yourself is not always easy, and it certainly can be lonely some of the time. But loving who you are is like a muscle: the more you work it, the stronger it gets. It's all about becoming your own bestie. Be authentic no matter what!

"Nothing can dim the light that shines from within."

—MAYA ANGELOU

4 THINGS YOU CAN DO TO STAY AUTHENTICALLY YOU!

- Do what makes you happy, even if you have to do it alone.
- Don't be pressured by trends or your peers to be something you are not.
- Give yourself compliments when you do kind things for yourself.
- Listen to your heart no matter what is happening around you.

SO YOU'RE TELLING ME THIS BECAUSE...?

It's super easy to do things that are not authentic to who you really are so that other people will like you or think you are cool. No one wants to be left out. You might do stuff to impress someone or show off, even when you know deep down inside "this is not who I really am." Don't become part of the pack. There is only one of you! Do you know how special that is? When you are not being truly you, you have stepped out of your power zone. Your authentic power lies in being connected to your HeartStar and being proud of the person you are, no matter what anyone else says or feels.

FOR Reals?!

ACTIVITY ⚠️ ALERT
Me, Myself & I

What does your authentic self look like? It's not who you see when you look in the mirror, but rather who you truly are inside. Create a True Self Portrait of who you really are inside. Dig deep and find whatever represents the true you. Have fun, and be as creative and free as you possibly can.

SUPPLIES

- Piece of paper
- Scissors
- Old magazines
- Glue stick
- Pens, pencils, crayons, markers, or paint

Use whatever you want! There are no rules!

Step 1	Step 2	Step 3	Step 4

Fold paper in half, unfold, and cut into 2 equal pieces.

Take a few deep breaths to connect to your HeartStar.

Cut out inspiring words and pictures you relate to from magazines.

Draw, sketch, doodle & collage your True Self Portrait.

LOVE LETTER to Self

I love you because . . .

Dear Me,

I love you so much. Thank you for allowing me to be myself. I love that I am a kind person. I love that I help people when they need it. I love that I have good manners and always remember to be nice to others. I love that I am my own person and that I don't follow the crowd. I love that I am funny and smart. I love that I am creative and thoughtful. I love that I am ME!

XOXO ♥ ME

There are so many things to LOVE about who you are! Are you a kind person? Do you help others? Do you have hidden talents? Come up with 5 wonderful words about your authentic self and write them down. Then write a love letter thanking yourself for all the wonderful qualities that you love about YOU.

SUPPLIES

- The other half of the self-portrait paper
- Pen or pencil
- Tape or glue stick
- Your True Self Portrait

Step 1

Write a love letter to yourself!

Step 2

Glue-stick or tape the back of your letter to the back of your portrait.

Step 3

Every night for 1 week, right before you go to bed, read your letter out loud in front of the mirror.

Step 4

Take a final moment to close your eyes and thank your true self for being you. ♡

S.O.A. MOMENT

QUESTIONS TO PONDER

- Am I a kind person?
- Do I keep my word when I make a promise?
- Do I help when other people need me?
- Do I use a gentle voice with myself? Or do I criticize myself?
- Do I give myself compliments when I do something well?
- Do I express my honest feelings?

AUTHENTIC POWER / TRULY YOU

SAY THIS:

I am complete.
All that I need already lives inside me.
I have a strength no one can touch, a light that no one can turn off.
My true self shines bright and I will let the world see me!

ANSWER THIS:

I believe I know my true self
  a. a little
  b. pretty well
  c. very well
  d. 100%

FILL IN THE BLANKS:

1. I feel most myself when I am _____.

2. The best I have ever felt about myself is when I _____.

3. Being authentically me means that I love myself just as I am. It means embracing my flaws. Two of my flaws that I have a hard time with are _____ and _____.

4. I believe I can work on these flaws by _____.

5. I am imperfectly beautiful. When I am authentic, I accept all of myself. The thing I love most about being me is _____.

6. Five words to describe my authentic self are _____, _____, _____, _____, and _____.

SIGN THIS:

I promise to spend more time letting my true self show.

_____   _____
Signature   Date

S.O.A. TOOL KIT
with love letter added

NATURE IS MAGICAL

CHAPTER FOUR

Did you know you have magic at your fingertips — in fact, it surrounds you? There is no greater evidence of a higher force than nature. Nature is an amazing teacher because it knows exactly what to do and when to do it.

By *nature* we mean plants, trees, and flowers that grow from the earth, and things like the oceans, lakes, mountains, sky, and animals that are part of our planet. Without resisting, nature goes with the flow. Nature adapts and changes in organized chaos. You could even say that nature IS change — it flows constantly from one thing to the next.

Have you noticed how calm a tree is through the seasons of change? No matter what is happening around a tree, there is a stillness that comes from the tree being rooted in the ground. During each season, change is taking place. In winter the tree is in the cold with no leaves and remains rooted in stillness. In the spring, the tree blossoms with vibrant leaves and sometimes flowers and keeps that same stillness. Even in the summer when there is not much water the tree remains rooted. Nature is always inviting us to be students of acceptance. Nature bestows the gift of learning how to embrace change. Just by watching a tree through the seasons we can establish trust in the journey of our own lives.

FACT In various studies, walks in nature have been linked to enhanced mental health and a positive attitude. These studies suggest that walking outside in a natural setting might help reduce feelings of stress and depression.

"When the roots are deep, there is no reason to fear the wind."
—PROVERB

Nature teaches us that no matter what comes our way, we have the ability to overcome obstacles and face fearful situations and come out on the other side stronger.

What a great lesson to learn! Nature is a true gift. Anytime we feel disconnected from our true selves, nature reminds us how to return to that space inside that is adaptable. At School of Awake, we go beyond what nature offers us and we remember that nature needs our love, our attention, and our admiration, too. When we are unkind to nature, we are being unkind to ourselves.

It's no secret our planet is suffering. Science has proved that our environment is under great threat because of the way humans treat the earth and animals. Remember, we are all connected. What we do to nature, we do to ourselves. We have nearly exhausted nature's bountiful resources, and that reflects our greed as well as our lack of awareness of our interconnection with nature. When we humans learn to love ourselves, we will become more loving to others and make choices that are kind to Mother Earth and all her creatures.

THE MAGIC OF NATURE'S ELEMENTS

The moon, the sun, the ocean, the sky, and the very ground you stand on are potent elements of our planet. For centuries, in all cultures around the world, people have worked with nature to find or grow food to eat, create art from rocks and plant fibers, and live well in their environment, such as by building homes out of snow or on stilts over water. We have fallen out of synchronicity with nature. Our busy modern lives and the distractions of technology have gotten in the way of our relationship to ourselves and nature.

BE ROOTED

BE STILL

CALM

BE HERE NOW

GO WITH THE FLOW

"Our ancestors worshipped the sun and they were far from foolish. It makes good sense to revere the sun and the stars, because we are their children."
—CARL SAGAN

Nature holds messages for us when we get quiet and become present. When we observe nature, we can respect a power higher than ourselves. Nature is one thing humans cannot control, and it is a living, moving, shifting force that is bigger and stronger than all of us. When we develop the connection between ourselves and nature, we can invite in our natural courage to deal with any obstacle that comes our way.

"Those who contemplate the beauty of the earth find reserves of strength that will endure as long as life lasts."
—RACHEL CARSON

SURPRISING WAYS NATURE HELPS HUMANS

- Studies show nature can strengthen our immune systems.
- Being in nature after a stressful situation can boost endocrine hormones that produce a calming effect in our brains.
- Having even a small plant in a hospital or office has been proven to reduce stress levels.
- Many health cures and antibiotics come from nature.
- The rain forest holds more than 170,000 plant species, and many of them may be used to cure disease in the future.

RACHEL CARSON was a biologist who is considered the founder of the environmental movement. She grew up on a farm, surrounded by animals and nature, and also loved, studied, and wrote about the ocean. She is best known for studying the way the pesticide DDT — used to kill the insects that harm farm crops — hurt the environment and made people and animals sick. Her classic 1962 book on this subject — called *Silent Spring* because of the way pesticides killed birds and made the spring "silent" without their song — brought the issue to popular attention. Although her work was attacked by the chemical industry, Carson defended her facts before the U.S. Senate, and DDT was banned in the United States in 1973.

Nature has existed from the beginning of time. When we observe the organized chaos that is happening in nature, we can become inspired by nature's radiance.

"We need to find God, and he cannot be found in noise and restlessness. God is the friend of silence. See how nature — trees, flowers, grass — grows in silence; see the stars, the moon, and the sun, how they move in silence. . . . We need silence to be able to touch souls."

—MOTHER TERESA

NATURE'S ELEMENTS FUN FACTS

- The moon controls the tides of the ocean.
- Since our bodies are mostly water, we are also connected to the moon.
- Remember that the sun is a star and is made of stardust, just like you!

THE SUN AND THE MOON ARE THE MOST DEPENDABLE FORCES YOU WILL EVER HAVE IN YOUR LIFE. No matter what else changes, the sun will rise and the moon will move through its cycles. Without fail, over and over. That's what we call trust.

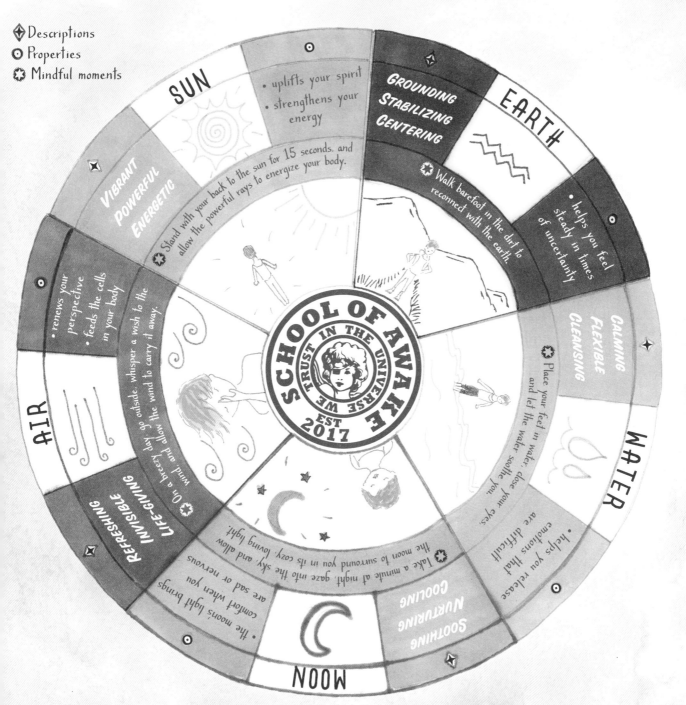

Descriptions
Properties
Mindful moments

SUN

- uplifts your spirit
- strengthens your energy

VIBRANT POWERFUL ENERGETIC

Stand with your back to the sun for 15 seconds, and allow the powerful rays to energize your body.

EARTH

GROUNDING STABILIZING CENTERING

- helps you feel steady in times of uncertainty

Walk barefoot in the dirt to reconnect with the earth.

AIR

- renews your perspective
- feeds the cells in your body

REFRESHING INVISIBLE LIFE-GIVING

On a breezy day, go outside, whisper a wish to the wind, and allow the wind to carry it away.

WATER

CALMING FLEXIBLE CLEANSING

- helps you release emotions that are difficult

Place your feet in water, close your eyes, and let the water soothe you.

MOON

- the moon's light brings comfort when you are sad or nervous

SOOTHING NURTURING COOLING

Take a minute at night, gaze into the sky, and allow the moon to surround you in its cozy, loving light.

SCHOOL OF AWAKE
WE TRUST IN THE UNIVERSE
EST 2017

SOME OF NATURE'S GIFTS FROM A TO Z

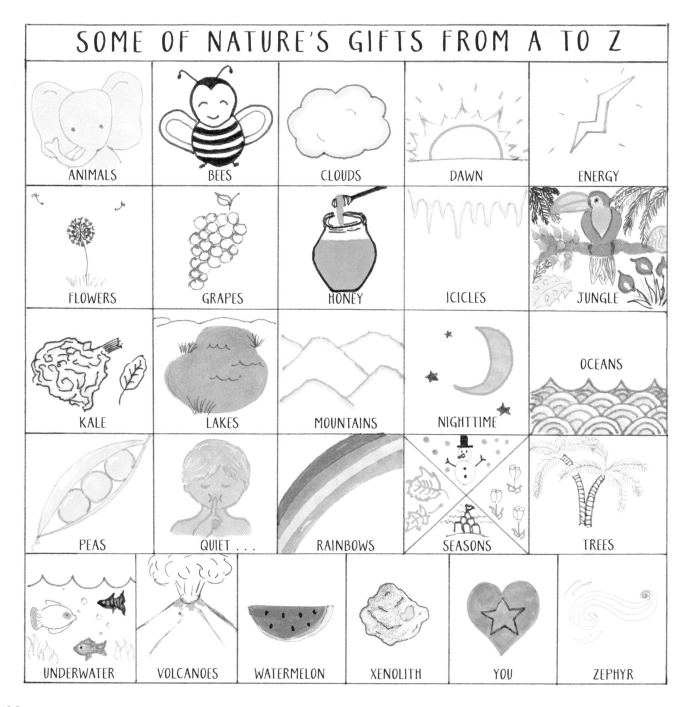

ANIMALS	BEES	CLOUDS	DAWN	ENERGY
FLOWERS	GRAPES	HONEY	ICICLES	JUNGLE
KALE	LAKES	MOUNTAINS	NIGHTTIME	OCEANS
PEAS	QUIET . . .	RAINBOWS	SEASONS	TREES
UNDERWATER	VOLCANOES	WATERMELON	XENOLITH	YOU	ZEPHYR

ACTIVITY  ALERT
Love Is All Around

LET'S GO ON A SCAVENGER HUNT FOR HEARTS!

Nature has sprinkled us with little reminders of love. Head outside and explore your surroundings. Be on the lookout for hearts — they're everywhere! They're in the leaves, clouds, water, rocks, and everything in between. Pretty soon you'll see them every time you leave your home!

STEP 4

Use a photo app to make a collage, or glue your drawings into a collage, and take your ♡s everywhere you go.*

* Add a small heart-shaped piece of nature to your tool kit.

STEP 3

Snap a photo or draw a picture to document the ♡ you found.

STEP 2

When you find a ♡ take a moment to appreciate it.

STEP 1

Go outside & explore.

"Forget not that
the earth delights
to feel your bare
feet and the winds
long to play with
your hair."

—KHALIL GIBRAN

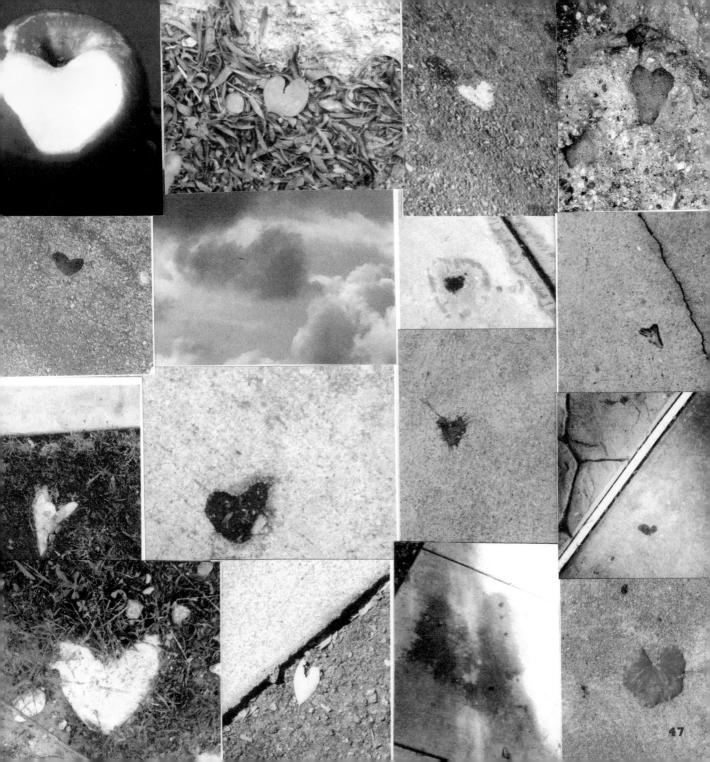

WAYS TO DRAW ON NATURE'S POWER

- When you feel sad or nervous, you can gather support from the moon. Feeling its nighttime coolness will move you toward calm.
- The sun is fiery and powerful. It lights up the planet every day, without fail. When you feel excited or low on energy, thank the sun for its vibrancy and joy.
- The earth nurtures plants and trees through roots that grow deep down into the soil. Trees grow from these roots and give us oxygen to live and breathe. When you feel wobbly in your life and a bit unsure of things, ask the earth below your feet to ground you and support you, just as it does the trees.
- The ocean is filled with more history than all the museums in the world put together. The plants that grow in the ocean produce 50 percent of the world's oxygen. When you need soothing and peace of mind, you can put your feet in water or envision the ocean and ask for her flexibility and cleansing.

Nature is magical, and these amazing gifts
from nature are free and here for everyone!

SO YOU'RE TELLING ME THIS BECAUSE...?

Nature sprouts up everywhere, even through cracks in the pavement. Just look up at the miracle of a huge blue sky or down at colorful, fragrant flowers that grow from the ground. Even weeds grow in the worst circumstances, not giving up, demanding to be acknowledged. Without nature, we wouldn't have oxygen to breathe or water to drink. All of these miraculous pieces of beauty happen right under our noses. Wow! Why do we overlook nature?

When we find the love we have inside for ourselves, we will learn to treat nature and animals with the love and respect they deserve. Nature has loved and supported us, and it's time we show our love and respect to the only place we can call home: Earth.

SNACK ALERT

HAIL TO THE KALE

The Royalty of All Veggies

INGREDIENTS

- 1 bunch kale
- Olive oil
- Garlic salt
- Garlic powder

FROM THE SCHOOL OF
AWAKE KITCHEN

DIRECTIONS

Preheat the oven to 300°F. Remove the thick stem from each kale leaf. Clean and dry your kale well. Cut the leaves into smaller pieces. Place the kale in a bowl and drizzle with enough olive oil to coat all the kale. Use your hands to make sure the oil gets on every piece. Sprinkle garlic salt and garlic powder all over your kale. Place the kale on a baking sheet in a single layer. Bake at 300°F for 20 to 30 minutes, turning the leaves halfway through. Bake until crispy.

THE NATURE OF CHANGE

Just as nature is always in motion, so are our lives. Change is something that we have to become comfortable with. Seasons come and go, and the same way nature adapts to its constantly shifting environment, we also have to adjust to change. Embracing the cycles of nature can teach us to be allowing of the circumstances, people, and things that enter and exit our lives. As the leaves fall away from a tree in the fall, new flower buds blossom in the spring. Most of us try too hard to hang on to things when they are leaving our lives, but we can learn from nature. After all, we are made of stardust! When we can accept change and release what is exiting our lives, we make room for the new.

"Earth is turning at more than 1,600 kilometers per hour while it orbits the sun at 100,000 kilometers per hour. And the sun is moving through the galaxy at a half a million miles per hour. And the Milky Way is moving through the universe at nearly one and a half million miles an hour. There is no fixed place in the cosmos. All of nature is in motion."

—NEIL DEGRASSE TYSON

FOR REALS?!

S.O.A. TOOL KIT

THE POWER OF YOUR WORDS

CHAPTER FIVE

Did you know that every word you speak carries a vibration? Your words actually create energy and reality. It's no secret that our words can either lift someone up or tear them down.

Have you ever noticed that when you hear kind words, you feel warm? Maybe your lips turn up in a smile or your toes tingle. Or has anyone ever said something negative to you and you literally could feel it hurt your heart? Think about how you feel when you put yourself down, too. There is an instant physical response from your body. This is why the words we choose to use toward others and ourselves are really important.

Choosing the right words matters. Take time before you speak, even after you hear something hurtful. Go back to breathing and mindfulness because those tools can help you stay aware of what you are actually saying and how you are saying it. They can help calm you and bring you back to your HeartStar when the words of others pull you toward pain. Breathe before you start to speak so you can be choosy with your words.

"Raise your words, not voice.
It is rain that grows flowers, not thunder."
—RUMI

GO AWAY YOU'RE UGLY
YOU SUCK WE'RE NOT FRIENDS
YOU'RE NOBODY
I CAN'T STAND YOU
GET OUT OF MY FACE UGHHH
No one likes you

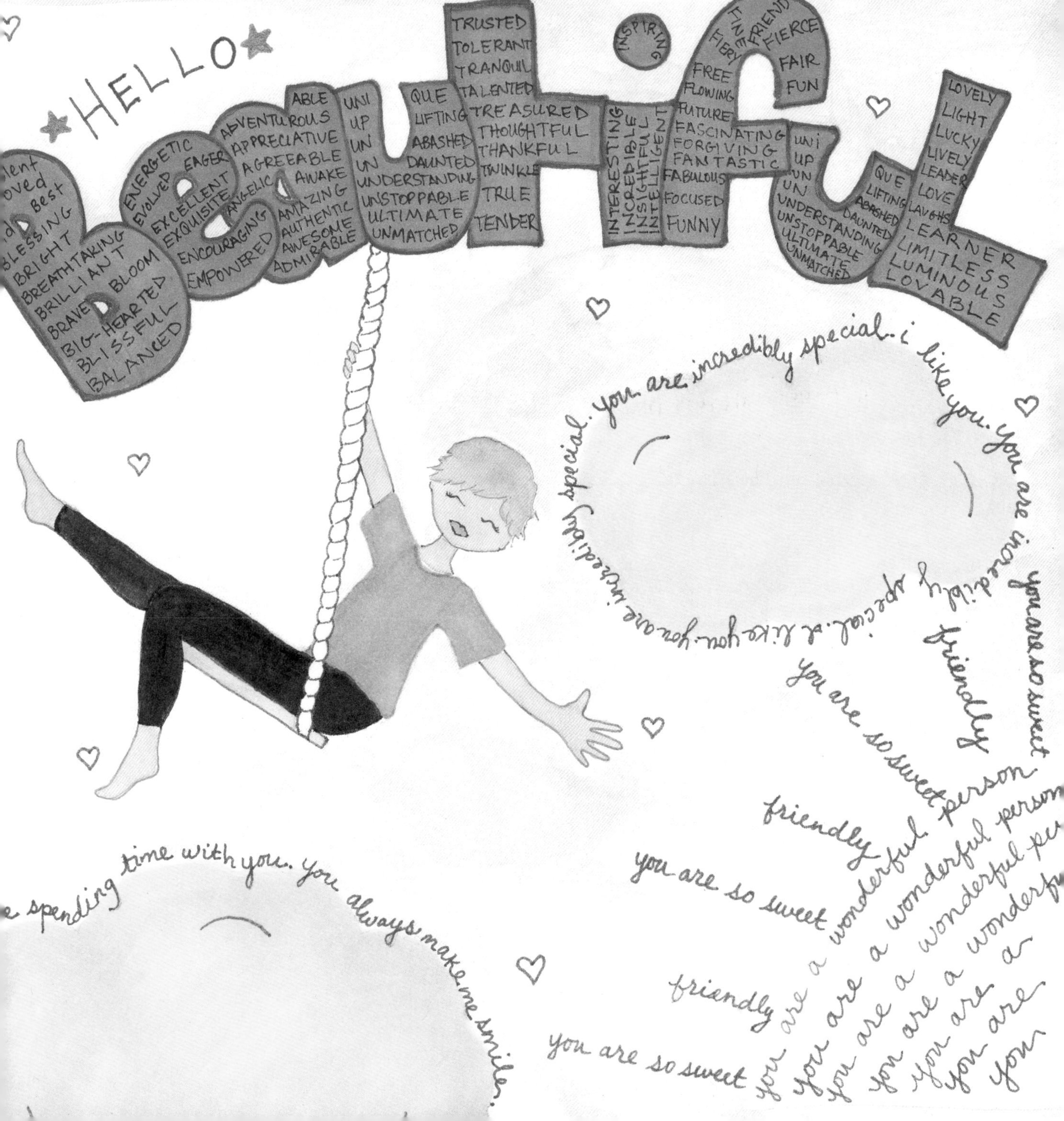

PLAY WITH THE POWER OF WORDS

SPEAK KINDLY TO OTHERS: Did you know that saying kind things to someone else can actually change how they feel? Pick 3 people every day to give an uplifting compliment to. Find something really kind to say to raise their spirits. See how they react and how it makes you feel. The compliment will feel good to the other person as well as to you.

PUSH THE PAUSE BUTTON BEFORE YOU REACT TO NEGATIVE WORDS: Being on the receiving end of other people's nasty words makes you want to be nasty right back. It's hard not to respond to someone's ugly words, but taking the mindful way of not reacting will make life easier for you. Do you want to be right, or would you rather be peaceful? And besides, haven't you sometimes reacted and then realized later that you'd misunderstood? Most of the time the battle is not worth the stress. Push PAUSE, take deep breaths, and sit with it before you react. Sit with your feelings to find the words to build peace rather than breed hate.

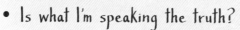

S.O.A. MOMENT

Ask yourself these questions before speaking:

- Is what I'm speaking the truth?
- Am I spewing words because I'm in a mood?
- Are my words hurting someone or uplifting someone?
- Could I find a kinder way to say what I'm feeling?

ACTIVITY ⚠ ALERT

The POWER of Words & Thoughts

Have you ever really thought about the science behind positive & negative words? S.O.A. has talked about how it feels when someone says kind or mean words to you, as well as how you feel when you speak and think positively vs. negatively. Here's an experiment that will actually show you the effects!

SUPPLIES

- 2 cups white rice (any kind)
- 2 glass or plastic containers with lids (such as spaghetti sauce jars or plastic food-storage containers) OR 2 glass or plast[...] containers, plus plastic wrap and 2 rubber ba[...]
- 2 labels OR tape you can write on
- Permanent marker
- YOUR WORDS & THOUGHTS
- Journal or notepad
- Camera (cell phone is fine)

STEP 1	STEP 2	STEP 3	STEP 4	STEP 5
	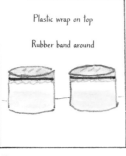			
Cook your rice and let it cool completely.	Put equal portions of the rice in the 2 containers. Seal with lids or plastic wrap and rubber bands.	Label container 1 "LOVE," label container 2 "HATE." Place them next to each other.	Think positive thoughts and say kind words to the "LOVE" rice.	Think negative thoughts and say mean words to the "HATE" rice.

Plastic wrap on top

Rubber band around

LOVE   HATE

DAY 1

DAY 7

DAY 15

END RESULT

STEP 6

Visit your rice a few times a day, especially when you feel happy or angry, and each time repeat steps 4 and 5.

STEP 7

In your journal or notepad, write down the words you say and the thoughts you have.

STEP 8

Keep track of the days and take pictures of your rice every 2 to 3 days.

STEP 9

Do this for 3 to 4 weeks. Watch as your rice changes.

At the end of that time, compare the "LOVE" rice with the "HATE" rice. Do they look different? The "HATE" rice will look ugly and moldy, while the "LOVE" rice may have a few spots on it but will mostly look white and fresher. What does this tell you about the power of your words and thoughts?

> *"Kind words can be short and easy to speak,*
> *but their echoes are truly endless."*
>
> —MOTHER TERESA

S.O.A. MOMENT

DO THIS:

1. Can you think of a time in your life when you said something kind to someone else and it made them so happy you could feel their joy?

   What did you say? _____
   _____

   How did it make you feel? _____
   _____

2. Now, can you think of a time when someone said something unkind to you?

   What did they say? _____
   _____

   How did it make you feel? _____
   _____

3. List 5 words that make you feel good: _____, _____, _____, _____, _____.

Say the first word out loud, then close your eyes. Create a picture in your mind for the word, and really feel it. Do this with each word.

4. Now make a list of 5 words that feel super negative: _____, _____, _____, _____, _____.

Say the first word out loud, then close your eyes. Create a picture in your mind for the word, and really feel it. Do this with each word.

5. Did you feel a difference when you said the positive words vs. the negative ones?

When I said the positive words, I felt _____.
When I said the negative words, I felt _____.

PRACTICE THIS:

Today I will . . .
- ☐ Smile at 5 people I don't know.
- ☐ Give compliments to 3 strangers.
- ☐ Send silent good wishes to 7 people I walk by.
- ☐ Say thank you to 3 people in my life for something they have done for me.
- ☐ Make sweet mini notes for my friends and hide them in their backpacks or jacket pockets.

How did these good deeds make you feel? _____.
Which was your favorite to do? _____.
Will you do it again? _____.

WHAT IF I COME FROM A FAMILY THAT DOES NOT SPEAK KINDLY?

It's not easy to feel great about yourself if you are living in an environment that is not supportive. Not everyone has mindful family members. Sometimes the people we live with feel like strangers even though we are with them every day.

Day-to-day life can be a lot of work. It can be hard for a group of people to live together and understand each other all the time. Some family members don't always blend well together. Just as oil and water don't mix easily, sometimes family members can clash. The mix of personalities can be challenging, and it's always shifting with life's ups and downs.

Sometimes the people you live with may say things or do things that really hurt you.* Does that mean your family members don't love you? No. But family life requires adjustments. This is when you have to be extra strong and remember how wonderful you are. That's not easy, but it is a time to reconnect with your HeartStar.

Stay true to your authentic self. Try to stay focused on the good parts of your family, and return to your HeartStar to feel strong. Maybe go out to nature to feel how you can remain still and calm despite what happens around you. Always keep in mind: your own self-love is more powerful than you know.

"The words of the reckless pierce like swords, but the tongue of the wise brings healing."

—PROVERBS 12:18

* If you find yourself in a situation where someone is physically hurting you or harming you, stick up for yourself and get help.

Don't forget to breathe and come back to your HeartStar. Once you get there, you start to think of all the amazing things about you.

HATER BLOCKER

Creative visualization is a very powerful practice in which you use your imagination to picture something that you want to make into a reality. When we can visualize something in our mind's eye, our body often follows by feeling what we would feel in the moment when what we've pictured actually has come to be, such as happier or more relaxed. When someone is letting out all their negativity with aggressive, unkind words, you can use creative visualization to protect yourself: Imagine yourself in a tall rubber tube with the thickness of a tire that goes from below your feet to 2 feet above your head. Imagine every mean word you are hearing shrinking in volume,

making this mean voice sound high-pitched and small like a mouse's. Picture all the words bouncing off the rubber tube and not being able to touch you at all. Stand tall inside your rubber tube. Stay elevated in your authentic, HeartStar energy, and shake off the negativity.

AFFIRMATIONS: MAKE IT TRUE

Why not use words to build ourselves up! Now that we've learned that words carry so much energy, let's use them to elevate our mood and claim who we want to be.

An *affirmation* is a sentence we repeat over and over about ourselves that reinforces the positive things. It's a declaration that asserts who we are by focusing on the attributes we want to enhance. We repeat affirmations, knowing that they will come true. We can say them out loud, or we can write them down.

The best time to repeat an affirmation is first thing in the morning as we start the day. An affirmation like "I am going to do great on this test today" or "I have everything it takes to reach my goal" feels like a surge of good energy in our bodies and encourages us in the direction we wish to go. Good affirmations boost the positive and help us blossom into the lives we want.

When we speak positive affirmations about our lives and ourselves, we build confidence. When we are confident, we are powerful.

Always start your affirmation with "I AM" or other action words that are in the present tense, such as "I choose" and "I believe." That way, you are creating your statement in the present moment.

When you feel negative about something, try flipping it around by restating it as a positive affirmation. For example, instead of repeating to yourself, "Nothing ever works out my way," change it to, "My progress might be slow, but something great is around the corner."

How about you customize some daily affirmations that you can use to feel really good about yourself?

"Our intention creates our reality."
—WAYNE DYER

ACTIVITY ⚠ ALERT
AFFIRMATION FLAGS

STEP 1

Cut out five 2"-by-2" squares.

STEP 2

Decorate the squares.

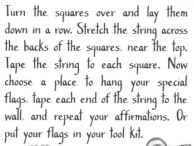

STEP 3

Write a different "I am" affirmation in each one.

I AM BRAVE

STEP 4

Turn the squares over and lay them down in a row. Stretch the string across the backs of the squares, near the top. Tape the string to each square. Now choose a place to hang your special flags, tape each end of the string to the wall, and repeat your affirmations. Or put your flags in your tool kit.

TAPE

TIME TO FEEL GOOD! LET'S LIFT OURSELVES UP BY THINKING OF SOME OF OUR BEST QUALITIES.

SAY YOUR AFFIRMATIONS WHENEVER YOU NEED A BOOST!

I AM BRAVE

I AM KIND

I AM CREATIVE

I AM FUNNY

I AM SMART

AFFIRMATIONS TO SAY TO YOUR REFLECTION IN THE MIRROR

I feel really good about who I am.

I am connected to my HeartStar.

I love being authentically me.

I am growing into someone I love and respect.

Life supports me and I enjoy being me.

I choose to speak words that are uplifting to myself and others.

I am getting better and better at doing things that once were a challenge for me.

I see myself improving in all areas of my life.

I have everything it takes to create the life I dream of.

I believe in myself and feel confident about myself.

I am beautiful just the way I am.

I am a unique, one-of-a-kind treasure.

S.O.A. TOOL KIT

"I choose to make the rest of my life the best of my life."
—LOUISE HAY

SO YOU'RE TELLING ME THIS BECAUSE...?

Words matter, and what you say to yourself and the people around you has a profound effect on how you feel and make others feel. When you are mindful, you create the space and time to pick the words that can make a difference for yourself and others. Use that power.

THE OCEAN OF EMOTION

CHAPTER SIX

Feelings! There are so many feelings inside each of us magical girls. Sometimes we are like the weather, changing direction in a split second. One minute we are overjoyed, the next we are holding back tears!

We are complex, beautiful beings, just like the elements of our planet. We experience what happens to us and around us, just like the earth experiences wind and rain and heat, and we're never sure what will come next. By nature, girls are sensitive and feel deeply. We are the life givers of this planet, so it makes perfect sense that we have such a wide range of emotions.

69

Sometimes our feelings are great motivators to get us to take action, and sometimes our feelings take over and put us in a mood that does not reflect who we really are. No one likes bad feelings such as sadness, anger, frustration, or low self-esteem. They just don't feel good in our bodies. When we learn to accept all our many feelings as passing weather, we tap into the strongest place inside us. We can feel our feelings, sit with them, and then let them go when we are ready.

Just think about a tree: No matter what is happening around it, it stays strongly rooted and is not affected by the weather surrounding it. It experiences the weather conditions, but it remains true to its tree nature.

When a rain cloud comes over the sky, it is big, dark, and heavy. Soon, though, that cloud passes. The sunshine comes back. Underneath all your uncomfortable, intense feelings is your true, joyful self. Sit with your emotions. Breathe into your intense feelings. They are important to experience, but you cannot let them steal your joy. Let your light shine through those dark moments, like rays of sunshine through the clouds. Your authentic, true self is there waiting to bring you back to love. Let the weather pass.

"Life is a series of natural and spontaneous changes.
Don't resist them; that only creates sorrow.
Let reality be reality. Let things flow naturally
forward in whatever way they like."

—LAO TZU

HAPPY

GLOOMY

ANGRY

SASSY

MYSTERIOUS

ANNOYED

THIS, TOO,
SHALL PASS...

Nothing in life stirs up emotions more than interactions with other people. In all the relationships in our lives — with people we have a crush on, bullies who are trying to put us down, friends we have fights with, our besties who make us feel at ease and at home — we strive for balance because our connection to others is what makes life worth living.

I HAVE A CRUSH

What is happening to us when we get all nervous around a certain someone we have a crush on? When we get butterflies and we can't sleep? It's like we become a different version of ourselves and start doing things we would not normally do.

When we have a crush on someone, our brain releases chemicals that make us feel and act this way. School of Awake likes to call this the "chemical cocktail." Attraction is a powerful force, and sometimes it can take us over in ways that make us forget our own needs. It's easy for cuteness to tell a lie. We create our own story about someone who attracts us, and it may not be accurate. Crushing is like wearing rose-tinted glasses: it colors everything and sometimes distorts what we see, leaving out parts of the other person. So how do we fall in love without losing our sense of self?

When your heart starts pounding for someone, remember to keep a part of yourself that is just for you. Try to build a foundation of friendship with the other person so you can get to know what they're really like.

Even when you meet someone you enjoy spending time with, you can't let go of your true self. When the chemical cocktail is in full effect is when it's most important to stay close to your HeartStar. Don't forget the bond you've created with your true self. Don't stop being who you truly are inside to make someone like you. When you are being the best version of you, the right crush will like you just the way you are.

THE ANATOMY OF A CRUSH

Levels of oxytocin, the "cuddle hormone," go up when you hug or hold hands with someone you like. (SMILE)

- Heart racing ✓
- Butterflies in stomach ✓
- Sweaty palms ✓
- Blushing cheeks ✓

YOUR BRAIN IS BUSY RELEASING A CHEMICAL COCKTAIL TO THE REST OF YOUR BODY.

Dopamine, or the "motivation molecule," is a chemical released when you feel a jolt of happiness (like when you see your crush). (SIGH)

Cortisol, the "stress hormone," and adrenaline, the "emergency hormone," are responsible for the excitement and nervousness you feel around your crush. (BLUSH)

SIGNS YOU ARE CRUSHING ON THE RIGHT PERSON

- You laugh together and feel like you are being yourself.
- You don't feel like you have to hide parts of who you are.
- You can share your weirdness and not feel judged.
- Your crush keeps their word and does what they say they are going to do.
- You are honest with each other.
- You have fun together.
- You are kind to each other.

If these things aren't happening, or if it feels one-sided (with you contacting your crush with no return calls or texts), or if the person hangs out with a big network of very attentive quote-unquote "friends," this may be a no-go crush. Relationships are about an exchange, and you should make sure it's a give-and-take, not all give and not all take. Back up. Look more closely. Are you being treated well? If you are tolerating behavior that you normally are not okay with, the chemical cocktail could be taking over. Think about people who treat you as you deserve to be treated. Crushing may feel great in the moment, but there is more to you than chemicals! Don't let your body take over without input from your brain and HeartStar.

SO YOU'RE TELLING ME THIS BECAUSE...?

One day you will fall in love (if you have not already) — at some point, the chemical cocktail is coming for you! Don't lose yourself and your integrity in the process. Relationships require a lot more than physical attraction. Keep your feet on the ground. Make sure you are being treated well and respected, and the give-and-take between you two is equal. Cuteness expires, while friendship and respect do not.

DO NOT GIVE YOUR POWER AWAY

LOOK FOR THE
LESSON

KNOW YOUR
SELF-WORTH

DO NOT
REACT

BE
HELPFUL

DRAMA-FREE
ZONE

BE
INCLUSIVE

STAY
MINDFUL

GO BACK TO YOUR
HEARTSTAR

LOVE
YOURSELF

DO NOT MIRROR UNKINDNESS

FISH FROM MY POND: CONNECTIONS

The challenging people we face are often balanced out by the people in our lives who we feel connected to. There is nothing like finding our people — our pod, our crew, our soul cluster, our squad! We feel kinship with them. They feel like fish from our own pond, and we love to be around them. They support and love us, and they share our sense of fun, our unspoken language, our likes and dislikes.

Some connections have seasons, and we need space from even our closest friends and family sometimes. That doesn't mean we won't come together again with them later. And sometimes connections with other people just expire. We grow in different directions, and things do not feel the same anymore.

Learning how to resolve arguments, misunderstandings, and even big fights with people you love is a crucial part of life. All of it is okay. Keep in mind that life is kind of designed to be uncomfortable at times so you can grow and learn. Be aware of your reactions, and notice when you're reacting from a place that isn't authentic. The more you know and love yourself, the easier your connections will become. To top it off, you will become your own best friend, the friend you can always count on.

4 TIPS FOR BEING A GOOD FRIEND

- BE A GOOD LISTENER: When your bestie needs a shoulder to cry on, give her all your attention. Sometimes a good venting session is all that is needed to feel better.

- BE UPLIFTING: Always find the positive about your friends. Remind them about all the wonderful traits they have. Lift them with kind words.

- DON'T BRING BONES: Don't be the bearer of toxic news to your friends. The truth always finds its way out. It's not kind to bring mean news to someone you care about, even when you think you are protecting your friend or being loyal.

- BE A GUIDING LIGHT: When your friends need advice, always lead them back to the choices that will make them feel good about themselves in the long run.

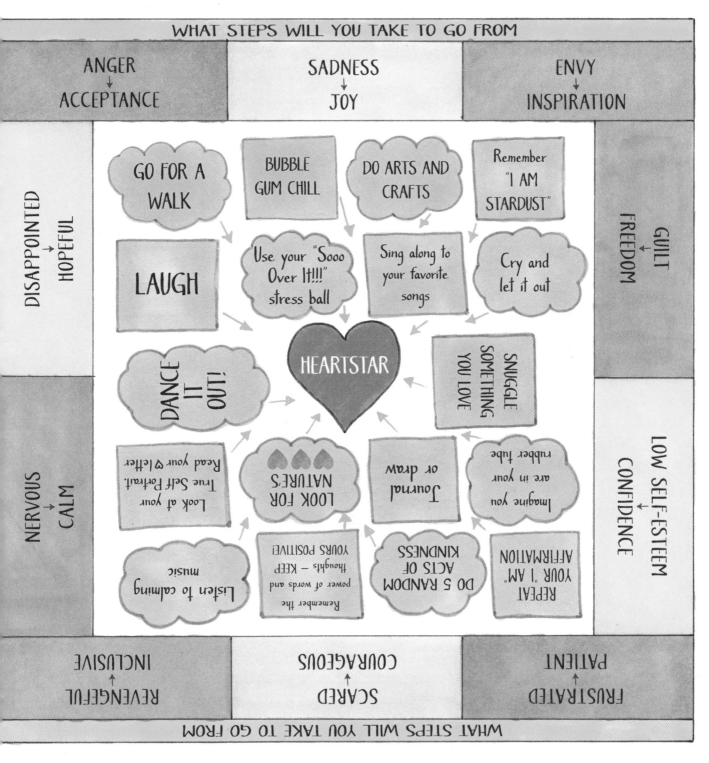

ACTIVITY ⚠ ALERT
Sooo Over It!!!
STRESS BALLS

Add your stress balls to your tool kit.

SUPPLIES
- Two 12-inch balloons
- Funnel
- 1 cup flour
- 1 pack water beads (available from dollar stores, craft stores, or online)
- Pencil
- Scissors

FLOUR STRESS BALL   ## WATER BEAD STRESS BALL

FLOUR STRESS BALL		WATER BEAD STRESS BALL	
1 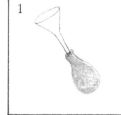	2 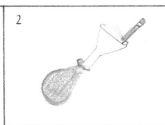	1 	2 
Insert the end of the funnel into the neck of the balloon.	Slowly pour the flour into the balloon. Use a pencil to help push the flour down and through the funnel.	Place your water beads in a bowl of water and set them aside to grow for 6–8 hours.	Insert the end of the funnel into the neck of the balloon.
3 	4 	3 	4 5 
Once all the flour is in the balloon, carefully remove the funnel and tie a knot.	Cut off the excess neck of the balloon, above the knot (be careful not to cut off the knot).	Slowly pour the beads into the balloon. Use a pencil to help push the beads down and through the funnel.	Carefully remove the funnel and tie a knot. Cut off the excess neck, above the knot (be careful not to cut off the knot).

ASSESS YOUR STRESS

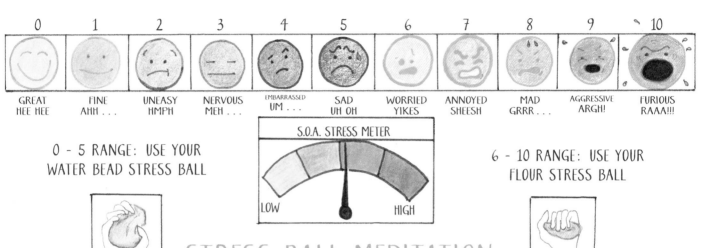

0	1	2	3	4	5	6	7	8	9	10
GREAT HEE HEE	FINE AHH . . .	UNEASY HMPH	NERVOUS MEH . . .	EMBARRASSED UM . . .	SAD UH OH	WORRIED YIKES	ANNOYED SHEESH	MAD GRRR . . .	AGGRESSIVE ARGH!	FURIOUS RAAA!!!

0 - 5 RANGE: USE YOUR WATER BEAD STRESS BALL

S.O.A. STRESS METER

LOW   HIGH

6 - 10 RANGE: USE YOUR FLOUR STRESS BALL

STRESS BALL MEDITATION

Inhale slowly while silently counting to 5. Hold it for 3 seconds, then slowly exhale while silently counting to 5. Repeat 2 more times.

Now think of a person or situation that makes you angry. Hold that thought!! Get mad! Think of all the reasons it was wrong and you are right! Feel that in your body.

While holding the angry feeling, start the slow breathing again. This time do it for 10 rounds.

After your last exhale, squeeze that stress ball as hard as you can, and hold for 5 seconds. SQUEEZE!

Release the ball and check in with your angry feelings. Not as angry, right? Maybe still a little steamy, but not as angry as when you started.

You can keep practicing this with any negative feeling. When you feel a feeling like frustration, sadness, or disappointment taking you over, breathe 10 rounds very slowly and then hold your stress ball and squeeze as hard as you can. Your stress level will go from a level 10 to a level 8 to a level 5 — just keep it up.

This puts you in the power position! No longer do you have to react to all your feelings or react to them every time they come up. Of course it's important to feel your feelings, but when you feel stuck, this is the tool to use!

WHAT TO DO AFTER A CONFLICT

- Cry if you have to.
- Take a shower or bath.
- Drink some water.
- Take several deep breaths.
- Let 24 hours pass before you make any moves (social media blocking, telling anyone else the details, swearing to never be friends again).
- Think of what you could have done differently.
- Think of the positive aspects of your friend and decide if you can forgive.
- Offer an apology if you need to, and ask for an apology if you need one.
- Don't be a hater.

It's really easy to look for all the things that are wrong about someone. Try to look for the positive.

WHAT IS A BULLY?

There is a difference between a friend who is annoying from time to time and a straight-out bully. Bullies are cowards who like to find vulnerable people to pick on and control. Deep down inside bullies hate themselves and feel powerless. Most bullies were taught how to be cruel by someone else in their family or friend circle when they were younger. When we're dealing with bullies, haters, and not-so-kind people, it's hard to remember that we're all made of stardust, but there are S.O.A. tools that can help!

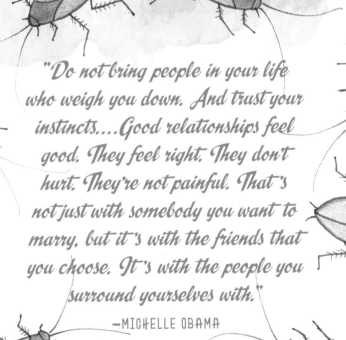

"Do not bring people in your life who weigh you down. And trust your instincts....Good relationships feel good. They feel right. They don't hurt. They're not painful. That's not just with somebody you want to marry, but it's with the friends that you choose. It's with the people you surround yourselves with."

—MICHELLE OBAMA

BULLYISH BEHAVIOR

- Using mean, hurtful words toward someone
- Physically harming someone or trying to control someone by invading their personal space
- Taking advantage of someone's kindness and mistaking it for weakness
- Ganging up on one person with other friends

BULLY FACTS

- Bullies are in pain.
- Someone has taught a bully mean behavior, or they would not know how to be a bully.
- Bullies are not happy people.
- Bullies are hiding their insecurity.
- Being a bully makes you weak, not strong.
- Bullies try to pretend they are cool and confident, but underneath it all they are weak and powerless.

ANTI-BULLY POWER AFFIRMATIONS

No one takes my power from me.
My happiness is not dependent on anyone's approval of me.
Mean people do not affect my self-esteem.
I deserve to be treated with love and respect.
My self-worth is not dependent on other people's opinions of me.

SHRINKY-DINK YOUR BULLY

If someone is bullying you, take all the power back from them by making them small in your mind. Picture them to be 1 inch tall, and imagine all the words that come out of their mouth sounding high-pitched, like a mouse's voice. Shrink them to nothing in your mind's eye, and they will lose their power over you.

There is nothing cool about being mean to someone. To protect yourself from bullies, find your true friends and stick with them.

S.O.A. MOMENT
BULLIES ON ICE

Write the first and last names of your bullies on separate small pieces of paper. Put them in a plastic bag and put the bag in the freezer. You've just created bullies on ice! Go to your HeartStar and breathe in and out for 1 minute with your eyes closed. When you are finished repeat this out loud:

My bullies have no power,
they are miserable inside
I choose to be a kind person,
where inner strength resides
I write your names on paper
and put you all on ice
All of you are frozen,
until you can be nice

FEELING UNITED IN A WORLD OF DIFFERENCE

Kindness comes from strength. When we are being our strong selves, we are naturally inclusive and kind to other people. People who have to make someone else feel bad about who they are in order to feel good about themselves do not understand their own self-worth. School of Awake teaches that some principles override differences, and these include love, kindness, sharing, tolerance, and equality. If we focus on these traits, we can work together and remain awake to possibility.

Tolerance means accepting others the way they are, but it does not mean we passively accept being treated badly. It means we stand firm in what we believe but we do not belittle others for what they believe. We remain open to differences while not tolerating bad behavior.

ACTIVITY ⚠ ALERT

S.O.A. Purpose Party!

SHARE HOPE & SPREAD LOVE

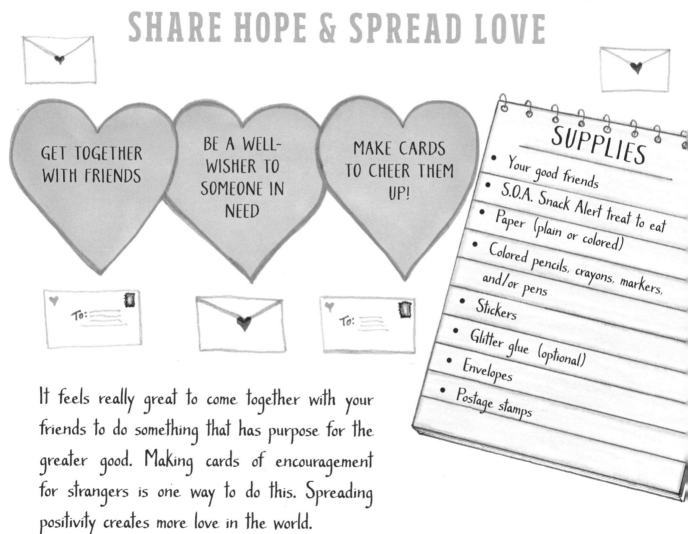

GET TOGETHER WITH FRIENDS

BE A WELL-WISHER TO SOMEONE IN NEED

MAKE CARDS TO CHEER THEM UP!

SUPPLIES

- Your good friends
- S.O.A. Snack Alert treat to eat
- Paper (plain or colored)
- Colored pencils, crayons, markers, and/or pens
- Stickers
- Glitter glue (optional)
- Envelopes
- Postage stamps

It feels really great to come together with your friends to do something that has purpose for the greater good. Making cards of encouragement for strangers is one way to do this. Spreading positivity creates more love in the world.

BRING A SMILE TO SOMEONE'S

HeartStar

STEP 1
Find a cause and their address to send your cards to.

- Children in hospitals
- Refugees
- Senior citizens' centers

STEP 2
Decorate your cards.

STEP 3
Write your messages.

STEP 4
Put them in envelopes, address them & stamp them.

STEP 5
Mail the cards.

DOS & DON'TS WHEN WRITING WORDS OF ENCOURAGEMENT TO STRANGERS

DO ✓
Use color and draw fun & happy cards.

DO ✓
Use inspiring quotes.

DO ✓
Write things like:
- Have a great day!
- Stay strong.
- You are amazing!
- I believe in you.
- You are incredibly special!

DON'T X
Write things like "feel better soon" or "get well" (some card recipients may be terminally ill).

DON'T X
Include any of your personal information like: last name, address, phone number.

WHEN THE GOING GETS TOUGH

There are going to be times in your life that are not easy. There will be times when everything feels lonely, unfair, and painful. This is part of life. As humans we experience the whole range of feelings and emotions, all as part of the journey of our lives. The point is to not let these hard moments take us down but to use them to build us up and help us grow. It's okay to fall apart and make mistakes. When we go through hard times, we get to know ourselves more deeply and become stronger. If we didn't learn the hard way, how would we make better decisions later in life?

So when the going gets tough, use your S.O.A. tools as much as you can, and when you feel like you are cracking into pieces, feel the new skin that is trying to grow underneath. You are resilient and capable of everything. Be soft and patient with yourself.

S.O.A. TOOL KIT

After every storm, the sun eventually returns, and you will overcome all your heart-aches if you are loving with yourself. Be brave! There is always a light at the end of the tunnel — and sometimes even rainbows!

SO YOU'RE TELLING ME THIS BECAUSE...?

Learning how to resolve arguments, misunderstandings, or big fights with people you love is a really important part of life. Ultimately, it's your own reactions and behavior you can control, not someone else's. Coming back together with a dear one after an argument can sometimes make your connection stronger. And sometimes closing a chapter with an outgrown connection moves us forward in our own growth. All relationships are great teachers that allow us to learn how to give and take.

YOUR SACRED SPACE

CHAPTER SEVEN

Your body is a sacred space. It's your mini universe and home to your HeartStar, remember? Your body is a gift you've been given in this lifetime, and it's your responsibility to take good care of it.

You wake up every day in your body. Your body moves, and you want it to feel good, so you have to be kind to it and make good choices about how you treat it. It reacts to what you put into it, what you think, and how you talk to it. The food you eat will change the physical aspects of your body for better or worse. The thoughts you repeat over and over, and even the smallest criticisms (or positive thoughts) you make throughout the day are messages to the body. All these things determine how you feel in your body.

Think of all the amazing work your body is doing for you during the day! Your heart is pumping, your stomach is digesting, your immune system is busy fighting off invaders, your skin is protecting you from environmental harms. All your body parts are doing the best they can to support you. Are you supporting your body?

Having a body is a gift. No matter what kind of body you have, it's beautiful! Being loving to your beautiful body means making mindful choices about what you put into it and how you use it.

HEALTHY THINGS MY BODY LOVES

89

HEALTHY FOODS = HAPPY YOU

7)

1)

2)

6)

3)

5)

4)

FOODS TO LIMIT

WHITE SUGAR

CHIPS

SODA

HYDROGENATED OIL
(A.K.A. TRANS FATS)

THINGS WITH MORE THAN 5 INGREDIENTS THAT YOU CAN'T PRONOUNCE

 1) HEART

Almonds, asparagus, avocado, blueberries, dark chocolate, oatmeal, salmon, walnuts

 2) BRAIN

Beets, bell peppers, cashews, celery, curry powder, dark chocolate, olive oil, peas, red meat, walnuts

3) SKIN

Blueberries, broccoli, cucumbers, oranges, salmon, spinach, strawberries, sweet potatoes, water

 4) EYES

Almonds, bell peppers, blueberries, carrots, kale, pumpkin, salmon, spinach, strawberries

5) IMMUNE SYSTEM

Almonds, apples, apricots, blueberries, coconut oil, garlic, ginger, grapefruits, lemons, raspberries, turmeric

 6) ENERGY BOOST

Bananas, brown rice, cashews, chicken, dark chocolate, kale, oranges, peanut butter, sweet potatoes

 7) HAIR

Almonds, avocado, beans, eggs, Greek yogurt, salmon, spinach, sweet potatoes, walnuts

SNACK ALERT

Girlie Glow Pops

FROZEN YOGURT TREATS THAT NOURISH YOU FROM THE INSIDE OUT!

RECIPE MAKES 4 POPS

FILLED WITH
• PROBIOTICS
• ANTIOXIDANTS
• PROTEIN

FILLED WITH
• CALCIUM
• MAGNESIUM
• B12

SUPPLIES

- 4 mini paper cups
- 4 Popsicle sticks
- Large bowl for mixing
- Blender (for blended Glow Pops only)
- Small spoon

INGREDIENTS

- 1 heaping cup plain Greek yogurt
- 1 tablespoon honey
- 1/2 cup frozen blueberries
- 1 cup granola, crushed

DIRECTIONS

1. FOR SWIRLED GLOW POPS: In a bowl, mix together the yogurt and honey. Add the blueberries and lightly stir to create swirls in the yogurt.

   FOR BLENDED GLOW POPS: In a blender, blend the yogurt, honey, and blueberries together until smooth.

2. Using a small spoon, layer the following into each cup: yogurt mixture, 2 spoonfuls of granola, more yogurt mixture, 2 spoonfuls of granola, and finish with more yogurt mixture.

3. Gently insert a Popsicle stick into the middle of each filled cup. Put them in the freezer for 4 to 6 hours or overnight.

4. Once they're frozen, slowly tear off the paper cups and enjoy your sweet treats!

HAPPY MIND, HAPPY BODY

Scientists are currently studying the ways in which a happy mind makes a happy, healthy body. They've discovered links between having a good mental attitude and fewer colds, for example. Focus on being upbeat and positive, and you might feel better physically, too!

Most of the time our bodies respond to our feelings. When we feel excited, sad, or nervous, we can feel all these things in our bodies. So what we are thinking will affect what we are feeling, which then affects our bodies and our choices. Staying mindful of our thoughts will help us navigate the ocean of emotions, and that will help our bodies remain peaceful and healthy. We always want to ask ourselves, "What is the kindest decision I can make for my body right now?"

HEALTHY EATING TIPS

- Drink water when you're hungry. Sometimes dehydration makes us feel like we need to eat.
- Try to have small healthy snacks between meals to keep your energy levels even.
- Breakfast is important, and be sure it includes some good protein.
- Choose a piece of fruit instead of a sugary snack.
- Choose balanced meals using fresh foods, such as vegetables and fruits, as much as possible, and eat food from bags and boxes less often.
- When indulging in processed foods, make sure to combine them with whole foods, such as avocados, apples, berries, spinach, and nuts, when you can.

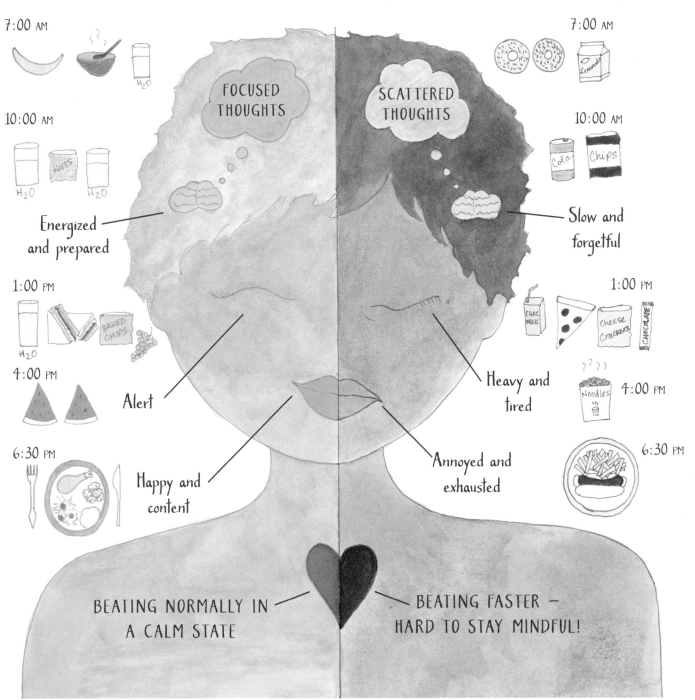

TALKING TO OUR BODIES

Our bodies respond to physical things, such as the food we eat and the exercise we do, and they also respond to our thoughts and what we say to them. When we have a thought, the cells inside our bodies respond. We can create positive thoughts to nourish and support our bodies, just like we can drink plenty of water and choose healthy foods. We want our thoughts and what we say to our bodies to encourage them to feel safe and loved.

No matter what state your body is in, you have the power to speak loving and kind words to your body.

Lotus pose

I AM PEACEFUL

Boat pose

I AM BALANCED

Warrior 2 pose

I AM STRONG

Tree pose

I AM GROUNDED

Downward dog pose

I AM CONNECTED

PAUSE
RESET

🕉

Cobra pose

I AM OPEN

Gate pose

I AM FLEXIBLE

10 YOGA POSES
THAT RESTORE BALANCE & PEACE

Bridge pose

I AM CENTERED

Half moon pose

I AM FREE

Child's pose

I AM SAFE

95

5 KIND THINGS TO SAY TO YOUR BODY EVERY DAY

- I love my body and my body loves me.
- There are so many things I like about my body, and I'm working on making it stronger all the time.
- My body is healthy and beautiful just the way it is.
- I listen to my body and feed it healthy foods.
- I thank my body for loving and respecting me.

There are lots of kind ways to speak to your body. Think of your body as a dear friend: you would only speak to a buddy with encouragement and kindness, so talk to your body that way, too!

S.O.A. MOMENT

ARE YOU IN TOUCH WITH YOUR BODY?

1. Does your body feel different when you make healthy food choices vs. unhealthy food choices? If yes, list 3 ways your body feels different.
   a. _____
   b. _____
   c. _____

2. List 3 activities your body loves to do:
   a. _____
   b. _____
   c. _____

3. What is your all-time favorite healthy food?

4. What is your favorite unhealthy treat?

5. What is your favorite body part? Why?

6. What is your least favorite body part? Why?
   a. Do you speak unkindly about this body part? If so, how does it make you feel?

b. Can you practice speaking kindly to it? Write down a simple and kind phrase to say when unkind thoughts about this body part pop into your head.

7. Now, pick any body part you want and spend 1 minute thinking about all the things this body part does for you. Think about the ways it moves or works and how it interacts with your brain and the rest of your body.
a. Do you ever take this body part for granted?
b. Did you feel a little more connected to your body during that minute?
c. Are you feeling appreciative of all that this body part can do?

Regularly do this 1-minute body appreciation with different body parts to remind yourself of just how amazing your body truly is.

8. If you were to thank your body for all that it does for you, what would you say?

9. List 3 ways you could treat your body better:
a. _____
b. _____
c. _____

10. Write down where in your body you feel each of these emotions:
a. JOY: _____
b. ANGER: _____
c. SADNESS: _____

Once you have located where in your body you feel these emotions, focus on the feeling of JOY and practice transferring JOY into where you feel anger and sadness. Do this by breathing into these spaces, and then release the anger and sadness.

11. Finish the following sentences with 1 word that best describes what you feel:
a. When I am happy my body feels _____.
b. When I am angry my body feels _____.
c. When I am sad my body feels _____.

12. List 3 things that you do for your body (such as dancing, walking, eating healthy foods, napping, taking a hot shower) that always put you in a better mood:
a. _____
b. _____
c. _____

13. CELEBRATE YOURSELF! What is something unique that your body can do that not many others can do?

COMPARISON WILL STEAL YOUR JOY

All girls compare themselves to other girls. It's just part of human nature. We like to look at what other girls are wearing, what they are doing, their hair, their styles, what they have, and on and on. Then, automatically, we compare ourselves to others.

You have to remember: There is only ONE you. That's why you are special! You are one of one! Totally original with unique gifts! Why do we want to look like everyone else and have the same hair and face and clothes? Then we would all just turn into drones.

If we focus on who we are as a human being and what gifts and strengths we hold inside us, we won't want to be anyone else. I know it's hard because this world holds high beauty standards that we place value on. But looks change as we get older. We can't keep them the same. Looks are part of the world of form, and all forms dissolve. Anything you can touch will eventually change. The formless — what's inside you and what connects us all — is what does not change. So why not invest in your heart and your inner character? Become a beautiful person inside. What's inside is what you get to keep and also what you get to share. It's the brightest beauty life has to offer, and no one can take that away from you.

Competition keeps us separated. Connection brings us together.

SO YOU'RE TELLING ME THIS BECAUSE...?

It's boring when everyone looks exactly the same. Embrace your uniqueness. Focus on how you are different from others and how those differences make you special and rare. Do you really want to blend in?

STAR SLEEPER

One of the things that your body loves the most and that helps your body thrive is sleep! We're so used to pushing ourselves to the limit. It's not always easy to hear when our bodies tell us they are tired and need to rest. All bodies require sleep to be regenerated, so get it whenever you can, drifting off into a restful state to give your body what helps it function at its best.

The body loves to rest and recuperate to start fresh the next day. During sleep, your brain goes into a deep, restful state, releases the worries of the day, and falls into a place of recuperation and repair. During sleep, your cells heal and regenerate, your immune system renews itself, and your body and mind replenish themselves for optimum health. Sleep is like food for the brain, and you can feel free to indulge as much as you like!

THE DREAM WORLD

A lot happens in our sleep. Not only do our bodies get the rest they need and our cells rejuvenate, but our hearts and souls also go on a journey. Our sleep connects us back to our HeartStar through our dreams, where we have insights and visions about our waking lives. The dream world is like a whole other land that we travel to in the night.

Have you ever awoken from a nap or in the morning and felt as if you'd visited another planet, one that felt just as real as the one you woke into, just as real as your daytime life? If so, you know the potential power of your dreams. At School of Awake, we use sleeping dreams to connect to waking-life dreams and goals. Sometimes we are trying to work out our daily lives in our dreamscape, and sometimes feelings that we can't process while we are awake come out in our dreams.

"Without leaps of imagination, or dreaming, we lose the excitement of possibilities. Dreaming, after all, is a form of planning."
—GLORIA STEINEM

Have you ever dreamed about something and it actually happened the next day? Sometimes our dreams deliver messages of how to take the steps to get to the destinies we are trying to create. Our dreams can help us in our waking lives by weaving in our HeartStar's perceptions and interpretations, bringing us in touch with our deepest selves.

When you have a potent dream, a dream that stands out, make sure to write it down. Or draw it. Keeping a dream journal will help you recognize certain dreams that feel like they might be trying to tell you something. When you write or draw your dreams and then look them over, you might see that you are having a recurring dream that your HeartStar is asking you to look at. When a dream excites you, spend time with it. It could be your HeartStar leading you toward a dream come true.

QUESTIONS TO ASK BEFORE SLEEP

- What land do I want to visit tonight in my dreams?
- What do my dreams want to reveal to me tonight?
- What sign can I look for when I wake up as a message from my dream world?

"If your heart is in your dream, no request is too extreme."

—"WHEN YOU WISH UPON A STAR," SUNG BY JIMINY CRICKET IN *PINOCCHIO*

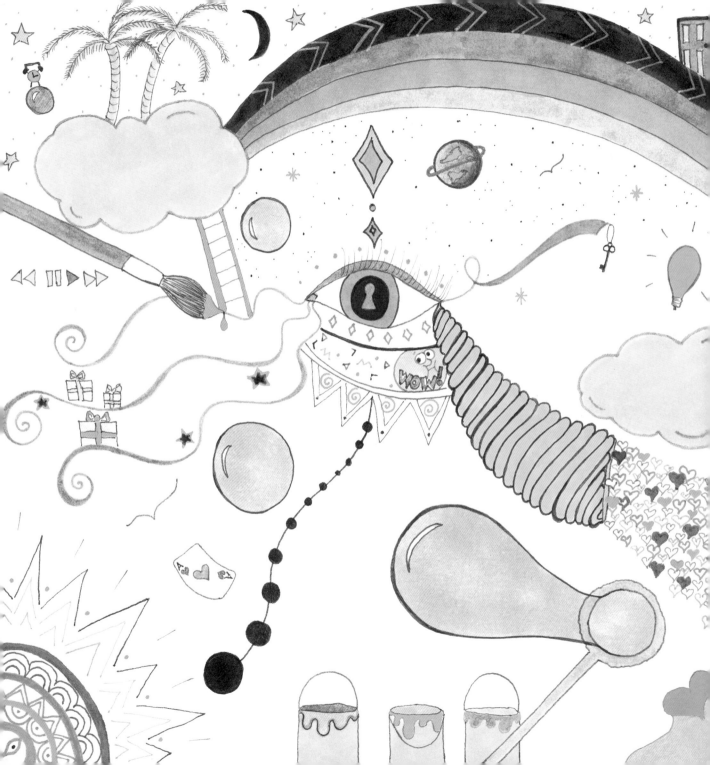

SLEEP HYGIENE

Just as we need to be aware of what we choose to put into our bodies, we also need to be conscious of what we do before we sleep. Sleep hygiene means making sure your sleep environment is free of the things that will rob your body of deep sleep. Here are a few tips for good sleep hygiene, which will make sleeping and dreaming even better for your body and mind.

TIPS FOR HEALING, REJUVENATING SLEEP

- Don't eat heavy meals late at night.
- Don't watch violent content on TV close to bedtime.
- Avoid looking at computer screens or phones for at least an hour before bed. (S.O.A. knows this is a tough one, but it really makes a difference.)
- Keep your room at a cooler temperature than during the day. Open a window to let in some fresh air, turn down the heat, or use your fan or air conditioner for 20 minutes to cool the room down before sleep.
- Practice mindful breathing before you fall asleep.
- Focus on positive thoughts before bedtime.
- Play relaxing music.
- Turn off your phone or set your phone to airplane mode before you go to sleep. EMF (electromagnetic field) waves can disturb sleep rhythms and get in the way of a great night's sleep.

By keeping your bed area uncluttered and tidy, you are destined to snooze off to a deep dreamland. One of the best beauty and health remedies we can give ourselves is good sleep!

ACTIVITY ⚠ ALERT

GIANT Dream Catcher

SUPPLIES

- 1 Hula Hoop
- 1 or more acrylic paints
- Paintbrush
- 1 doily (12-inch or smaller)
- Yarn or string
- Scissors
- Glue, hot glue, or tape
- Construction paper
- Pens, markers, pencils

OPTIONAL DECORATING SUPPLIES
(GET CREATIVE – USE WHAT YOU HAVE)

- Feathers
- Old fabric or T-shirts that you can cut up
- Beads
- Glitter

Dream catchers are believed to bring sweet dreams, good luck, and harmony. Native Americans traditionally made them and hung them where they slept so they'd have positive dreams and remember them.

Step 1: Paint your Hula Hoop. Let it dry. Add a second coat of paint if needed. If using more than 1 color, paint a design around your hoop.

Step 2: Lay your hoop on a flat surface. Place the doily in the middle of it. Use the yarn to measure the space between the doily edge and the hoop. Add 5 more inches of yarn to this measurement, then cut off that length of yarn.

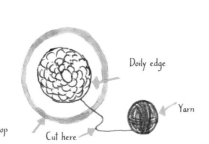

Doily edge

Yarn

Hoop

Cut here

Step 3: Cut 11 more pieces of yarn the same length as the first.

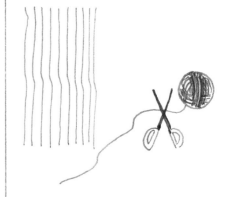

Step 4: Space out the yarn evenly around the doily.

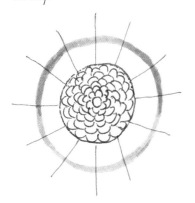

Step 5: Tie one of the yarn ends onto the doily's edge in a double knot. Do this for each piece of yarn.

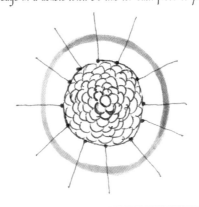

Step 6: Tie the other end of each piece of yarn around the Hula Hoop in a double knot. Cut off any extra yarn that is hanging.

Step 7: Cut 7 more pieces of yarn: 1 extra-long piece (about 18 inches), 2 long pieces (about 16 inches), 2 medium pieces (about 12 inches), and 2 short pieces (about 8 inches).

Step 8: Now comes the really fun part — decorating!!! Time to get crazy creative. Add whatever decorations you want to one end of each piece of yarn you just cut. Sky's the limit! You can draw and cut out symbols . . . or tie beads. You can tie or glue feathers. You can cut old fabric into strips. Starting at the center and working outward, tie the strings to the bottom of the Hula Hoop.

Step 9: Hang your dream catcher above your bed or nearby to bring peaceful sleep and sweet dreams. . . .

When our hearts have a wish, our whole bodies feel good. Instantly we smile and get butterflies in our stomach at the possibility of a dream coming true. School of Awake believes that making wishes is important. Wishes are the seeds to our dreams and destiny.

But wishes are not magic. They require more than just hope. We fuel our wishes by taking active steps and putting energy and extreme effort into the outcome. There is a staircase between a wish and a dream come true, and it can be steep and winding. Don't ever give up on your wishes no matter how exhausting the process is. When it seems like things are working against you and your wishes, remember that failure is part of success. We can learn from it. Think of failure as practice for succeeding. It's a journey up that staircase, so keep climbing and learning. Don't ever give up.

When you think about the people you admire, you'll realize they achieved their dreams by hard work, determination, perseverance, and faith. They didn't give up on their wish, and neither should you.

INGREDIENTS FOR A DREAM COME TRUE

PATIENCE	GOALS
PRACTICE	TIME
PERSEVERANCE	SURRENDER
TRUST	BRAVERY
LOVE	FAILURE
STRENGTH	S.O.A. SUPER POWERS
DAILY DISCIPLINE	

"Every great dream begins with a dreamer. Always remember, you have within you the strength, the patience, and the passion to reach for the stars to change the world."
—HARRIET TUBMAN

S.O.A. TOOL KIT

Wish Jars

SUPPLIES

- Jar with a lid (spaghetti sauce jars or jelly jars work great)
- Acrylic paints (as many as you want)
- Paintbrush
- Stickers
- Paper (plain or colored)
- Scissors
- Pens or pencils
- Thin ribbon (optional)
- Glitter and/or confetti (optional)
- "Smell-goods" — potpourri, lavender, rose petals, coffee, cloves, cinnamon sticks, perfume, or body spray (optional)

Step 1: Paint your jar and lid however you want: 1 color, patterned, your favorite symbols — whatever will make you smile. Let it dry.

Step 2: Decorate your jar with stickers.

Step 3: Cut the paper into wish strips. They can be small or big, depending on your wishes, but they have to be small enough to fit into your jar when rolled up.

Step 4: Write a wish on each strip of paper. Then roll them up into mini scrolls. If you have thin ribbon, you can tie a knot around each scroll.

Step 5: Place your completed scrolls inside your wish jar. Cover them with fun things: glitter, confetti, rose petals, potpourri, whatever you want. Choose 1, or mix and match your favorite combinations. And/or mist with your perfume or body spray.

Step 6: Close your jar, hold it tight, and wish a wish with all your might. Place your wish jar somewhere special, such as in your S.O.A. tool kit, so that every time you see it, you are reminded of all your amazing wishes.

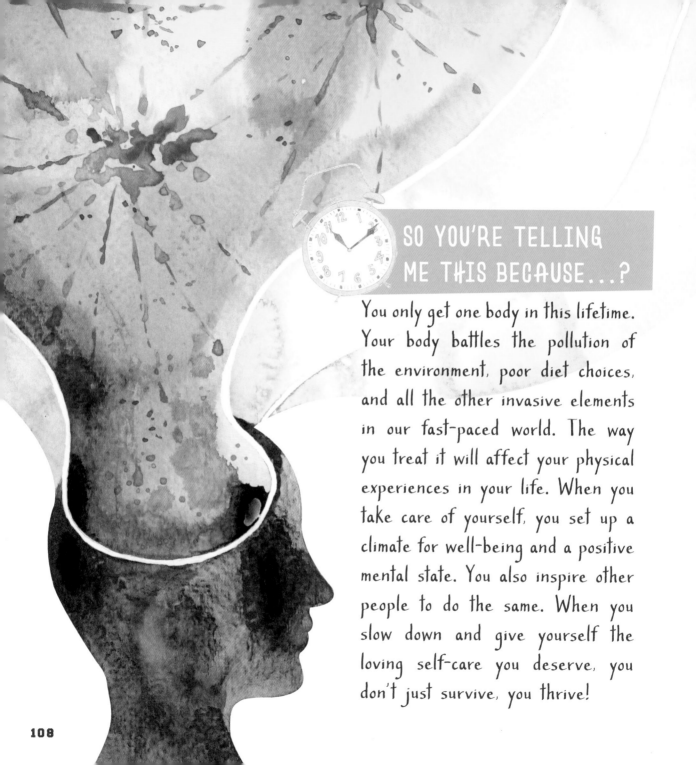

SO YOU'RE TELLING ME THIS BECAUSE...?

You only get one body in this lifetime. Your body battles the pollution of the environment, poor diet choices, and all the other invasive elements in our fast-paced world. The way you treat it will affect your physical experiences in your life. When you take care of yourself, you set up a climate for well-being and a positive mental state. You also inspire other people to do the same. When you slow down and give yourself the loving self-care you deserve, you don't just survive, you thrive!

YOUR SUPER POWERS

CHAPTER EIGHT

What are SUPER POWERS? Super powers are tools we hold inside that are invisible to the human eye. But just because you can't see and touch something doesn't mean it doesn't hold tremendous power. Think about music: you can't see it or touch it, but you can definitely feel it. Your super powers need to be practiced to get stronger. As with using any tool, you become more skillful the more you use them.

We call them SUPER POWERS because once you learn how to find, build, and use them, you'll discover they will help you get through a lot of different situations in your life. No matter who you are, life will give you challenges. Why not develop your super powers so you'll be ready to face anything that comes your way? They'll help you operate from a place of inner power, keeping you centered and strong, when life throws new experiences at you.

Here are some ways to go inside to gather your inner strength. Maybe one of these super powers stands out more than another, and that's okay. Or you might like all of them. Do what feels right for you. You will know which ones work best for you when you give them a try.

SOUNDTRACK TO YOUR LIFE

School of Awake loves music and believes music is a universal super power that touches all of our hearts and keeps us connected through the power of beats and melodies. Listening to your favorite jams will always bring you to your HeartStar. The way music moves us all teaches us how connected we are to each other, how deeply everyone feels rhythm, melody, and sound, and how much they can influence our feelings in the moment. You can play music in the background while you do your arts-and-crafts activities, and it will open the door for your creativity to flow.

EFT

School of Awake considers anxiety and panic 2 of the worst feelings in the world. What could be worse than feeling extreme stress in your body and not having any way to control it? *Emotional Freedom Technique* (EFT) is a practice of tapping on different acupressure points in the body to help cope with stress. Tapping encourages the nervous system to calm down and also balances the energy in the body. The technique was developed by modern psychologists based on ancient acupressure to help rewire the brain during times of stress.

HOW TO USE YOUR TRIPLE TAP POINTS

DO YOU HAVE...

FOLLOW THESE STEPS:

1. Focus on a specific emotion (anxiety, sadness, or stress). Rate the intensity of how you feel on a scale from 0 to 10, 10 being the worst.

2. Next, using your index and middle fingers, continuously tap on the karate chop point and repeat this 3 times: "Even though I have _____ [your emotion], I deeply and completely accept myself."

3. Move on to the 2nd point, at the beginning of your eyebrow (close to the bridge of your nose), and tap 7 times while you again say: "Even though I have _____ [your emotion], I deeply and completely accept myself."

4. Now tap 7 times on your rib cage point and repeat: "Even though I have _____ [your emo-tion], I deeply and completely accept myself."

5. Once you finish with all 3 tapping points, rate the intensity of your emotion again. Has it gone down?

6. If the intensity is still higher than you want it to be, go through the taps again. If tapping one point feels better than the others, continue to tap just that point until you reach 0 on the intensity scale.

TAPPING TO THE RESCUE!

3 PRESSURE POINTS THAT RELIEVE ANXIETY, SADNESS, AND STRESS

YOU CAN TAP YOURSELF TO A CALM SPACE!

USE YOUR INDEX AND MIDDLE FINGERS TO TAP ON EITHER YOUR RIGHT OR LEFT SIDE

TRIPLE TAP POINTS

2. BEGINNING OF EYEBROW POINT

1. KARATE CHOP POINT

3. RIB CAGE POINT

VISION ALCHEMY

Have you ever heard the expression "If you can see it, you can BE IT"? All goals start off as a small spark that is a vision. We sit with that vision and let it roll around in our hearts and minds until it becomes a dream we are ready to pursue.

Believing in a vision is powerful! Many of our heroes started with a single vision. Martin Luther King Jr. spoke about this in his famous speech "I Have a Dream." Harriet Tubman, a former slave, dreamed up ways to help other slaves escape to freedom on the Underground Railroad.

Has there ever been a time when you really wanted something to happen and you saw it play out in your mind in vivid detail, and then it actually manifested in your reality? School of Awake likes to call this *vision alchemy*. An alchemist knows how to transform the small things like ideas and visions into real-life experiences and tangible items. When we become mindful and focused, we are preparing fertile ground to hone our vision and begin the manifestation process. When you feel lost or confused about your vision, remember how you felt originally when you first had that magical spark.

School of Awake recommends you use vision alchemy to manifest uplifting, positive visions that benefit everyone. It's one thing to envision yourself being the most popular girl in town, but it's another to see yourself at the college you dream of, passionately succeeding and sharing your talents and gifts with the world. We leave it up to you, but visualize with awareness!

Don't underestimate a vision. You never know what you can do until you try!

One of the super powers we use to manifest our visions is called G.I.F.T.™, which stands for: go, intend, feel, transform.

GO: Go to your HeartStar. Sit somewhere quiet and peaceful, close your eyes, get quiet, and focus on your breathing.

INTEND: See the vision you wish to create. What does it look like? What are the details? Who is with you? What are you doing, and where are you? Make the vision of your intention as real as it possibly can be.

FEEL: Feel this vision. Feel it from the tip of your toes to the top of your head. Be in the dream! It's happening. As this vision manifests, what do you feel? Pretend it has come true, and feel every response in your body as though your vision has already happened.

TRANSFORM: Own it. Know it is coming. Transform into the version of you that you will be when this vision has already manifested. Act as if, and so it shall be!

You can always remember the word G.I.F.T. because when the manifestation comes true, you'll know you have received a gift!

GO TO YOUR HEARTSTAR.

INTENTION: SET YOURS AND SEE THE VISION.

Go
Intend
Feel
Transform

FEEL THE VISION.

TRANSFORM
INTO THE VISION.

G.I.F.T. COLLAGE

A G.I.F.T. collage is another powerful tool we can use to help manifest our visions. It's a small collage of things that inspire us and keep us focused on our goals and biggest dreams in a visual way.

There is something really cool about having a vision of your life and what you want to create, and mapping it out with arts and crafts. There are no rules here — this is your dream. Your collage will give the initial spark of your dreams fuel to go forward.

Here are some questions you can ask before you start:
- What do I love?
- What do I want to do when I get older?
- What makes me happy?
- What excites me about my life?
- What do I see in my future?
- What steps will I take to meet my goals?

Now that you have some inspiration for what you want to create in your life, you can express it in your G.I.F.T. collage. You can cut out images from magazines, glue or tape them to your collage, and use markers, pens, or stickers to add more words and images. You can draw directly on your collage, or draw and paste, or cut and paste.

There is no way to do this wrong. There is no perfect way, except the perfect way you choose! If you love the color blue, the whole board could just be blue! This is a NO-RULE project that is meant to make you feel good. This is a map to happy. When you look at your collage, you should feel joyful and inspired about your life and all its wonderful possibilities.

Once you finish your collage, sit with it daily in a quiet, mindful space and think about the steps you will take to create your dreams. As you sit with your collage, practice G.I.F.T. as described on page 114. Remember, everything starts as a small spark, and making a G.I.F.T. collage is a small step to a bigger possibility.

G.I.F.T. Collage

CREATE A MINI COLLAGE TO MANIFEST WHAT YOU WANT!

SUPPLIES

- Your S.O.A. tool kit
- Magazines
- Scissors
- Glue stick
- Markers, pens & stickers (optional)

What does your dream life look like? What kind of person are you? Go through magazines and cut out words, phrases, colors & pictures — anything that feels like you. ♥

Glue them onto the inside of your S.O.A. tool kit. Use stickers and markers to add even more detail. Create your ultimate mini dream collage.

Sit with your collage daily, and remember that it is a visual road map to help you create your dreams.

COLOR FORCE

How does color reflect or affect your mood? How do you pick out what you're going to wear every day? Have you ever noticed that on some days you're drawn to certain colors but you don't know why? We instinctively gravitate to colors that we feel connected to.

We all LOVE color, but I bet you didn't know that colors hold healing energy. Color can boost our mood and can have soothing properties. Scientists have shown that color influences our biorhythms and brain activity. Different colors bring out different feelings. Blue calms and soothes us, pink relaxes us, and red enlivens us. Some colors can bring us down, while others relax us or uplift us. We all respond differently to color.

Our eyes connect us to color. Color is made up of light and energy and enters through our eyes, then sends messages to our brains that can affect our state of mind.

School of Awake likes to use this mood-enhancing power of color to our advantage. That's why it's a SUPER POWER! Color healing is thinking of a color that makes you feel good and imagining yourself surrounded with that color, envisioning its light and energy healing and sustaining you.

If you visualize a color and surround yourself with it, you create a certain feeling. Imagine surrounding yourself in a delicious, soft, warm pink that starts at your feet and slowly moves up your body and eventually over your head. Nice, right? After a hard day, this pink would be a perfect nighttime cocoon to help you fall into sleepy dreams. Or let's say you're in a quiet mood and need space and solitude. Maybe you picture a bubble around yourself made of a soft gray color to protect your quiet space. Or if you are spending the day with your buddies, imagine a bright orange and yellow sunshine color surrounding all of you when you're together to represent warmth and joy. There are so many combos you can use, depending on what feeling you want to enhance.

You can practice this every day or just when you need an extra boost. Before long, you will know exactly what colors make you feel the best.

COLOR CHECK-IN QUESTIONS

- What color do I feel like right now?
- What color would bring a smile to my face?
- What part of my day felt great? What color does it make me think of?
- What part of my day do I want to forget? Does a color help describe it?
- What color can I pick to surround myself with to make sure today is a great day?

WHAT COLOR FORCE ARE YOU FEELING?

LOVING	INDEPENDENT	JOYFUL	COURAGEOUS	ROYAL	CALM
BALANCED	STRONG	NEW BEGINNINGS	CREATIVE	MYSTERIOUS	SWEET
AUTHENTIC	PLAYFUL	CARING	TRUSTWORTHY	GENTLE	FRESH
SUNNY	COMPASSIONATE	POWERFUL	WISE	DEPENDABLE	CONFIDENT
EXCITING	WARM	EARTHY	FRIENDLY	PEACEFUL	GRACEFUL
SMART	FLIRTY	ENTHUSIASTIC	LOW-KEY	ENERGETIC	SOOTHING

SCHOOL OF AWAKE COLOR CHART

CLOSE YOUR EYES & LET YOUR HEARTSTAR CHOOSE THE COLOR THAT SPEAKS TO YOU

MAY THE COLOR FORCE BE WITH YOU!

ENHANCE YOUR MOOD WITH COLOR!

COLOR IS ENERGY!

WAYS TO REMEMBER YOUR COLOR FORCE:

WEAR CLOTHES IN YOUR COLOR.

GO ONLINE. DO AN IMAGE SEARCH OF YOUR COLOR & TAKE A SCREENSHOT AS WALLPAPER.

JOY

COLOR IS HEALING!

ACCESSORIZE IN YOUR COLOR.

SURROUND YOURSELF WITH COLOR!

FINDING THE ZONE

Our minds are always busy, and it's easy to lose ourselves in too much thinking. Sometimes our minds just need a break, and we can rest them by going into the zone, which is School of Awake's other name for meditation.

The zone is where we find clarity and peace of mind. It's like going back to home base, where we are centered and quiet and in touch with our HeartStar.

Entering the zone is like pushing a PAUSE button on our thinking minds and finding a calm space within ourselves where everything becomes still and quiet. Once you get the hang of finding your zone, you become a nonreactionary Jedi, which means not much can knock you off your center. You keep your balance emotionally and become a master of being unaffected.

We meditate to rest our thoughts and our minds. It helps us to focus and become still.

Think of meditation as a nap for your brain. We close our eyes and focus on breathing in and out with long, slow breaths. Then, if our thoughts creep back into our minds, we watch our thoughts like a movie on a screen, witnessing them while we evenly breathe in and out. We let them flow, and they come and go.

Sometimes when we begin meditating, we find that we have way more thoughts and images going on in our heads than usual. That's okay. We just remain the mindful watcher and stay focused on how our breathing feels coming in and going out of our bodies. During your meditation, when you catch yourself thinking again, all you have to do is return your attention to the air flowing in and out of your body. You can also pick a color from the S.O.A. color chart and imagine that color moving in and out with your breath. Try it and see if it's helpful. With practice, you will find that a calmness comes over you and makes you feel very peaceful when you meditate. This takes practice. Just give it time and ride the wave.

HOW TO ENTER THE ZONE

Find a quiet space, dim the lights, and get comfortable. You can meditate lying down or sitting up, and over time you will get good at doing it anywhere! Close your eyes and then start with a deep breath in, followed by a slow, long breath out. Release the day and all the thoughts you might have. Now continue breathing, slow and steady, with your eyes closed. As you breathe in and out, you can visualize a color or you can repeat a phrase, such as "It's all good" or "All is well."

Continue inhaling and exhaling slowly. Focusing on the waves of breath will bring you to a place of stillness. Before you know it, you will feel a sense of calm, and your thoughts will have slowed down. Your body will relax. You've made it to the zone!

While you keep this up, your brain starts to release chemicals that calm your entire body. This strengthens your immune system, relieves stress, and helps to balance your emotions. It's the perfect way to start or end your day.

Finding your zone is not just sitting and meditating. It can also be losing yourself in your favorite activity — creating art, making music, writing, any creative space that you love being in so much that you forget time and space. That's the zone!

FINDING... THE ZONE

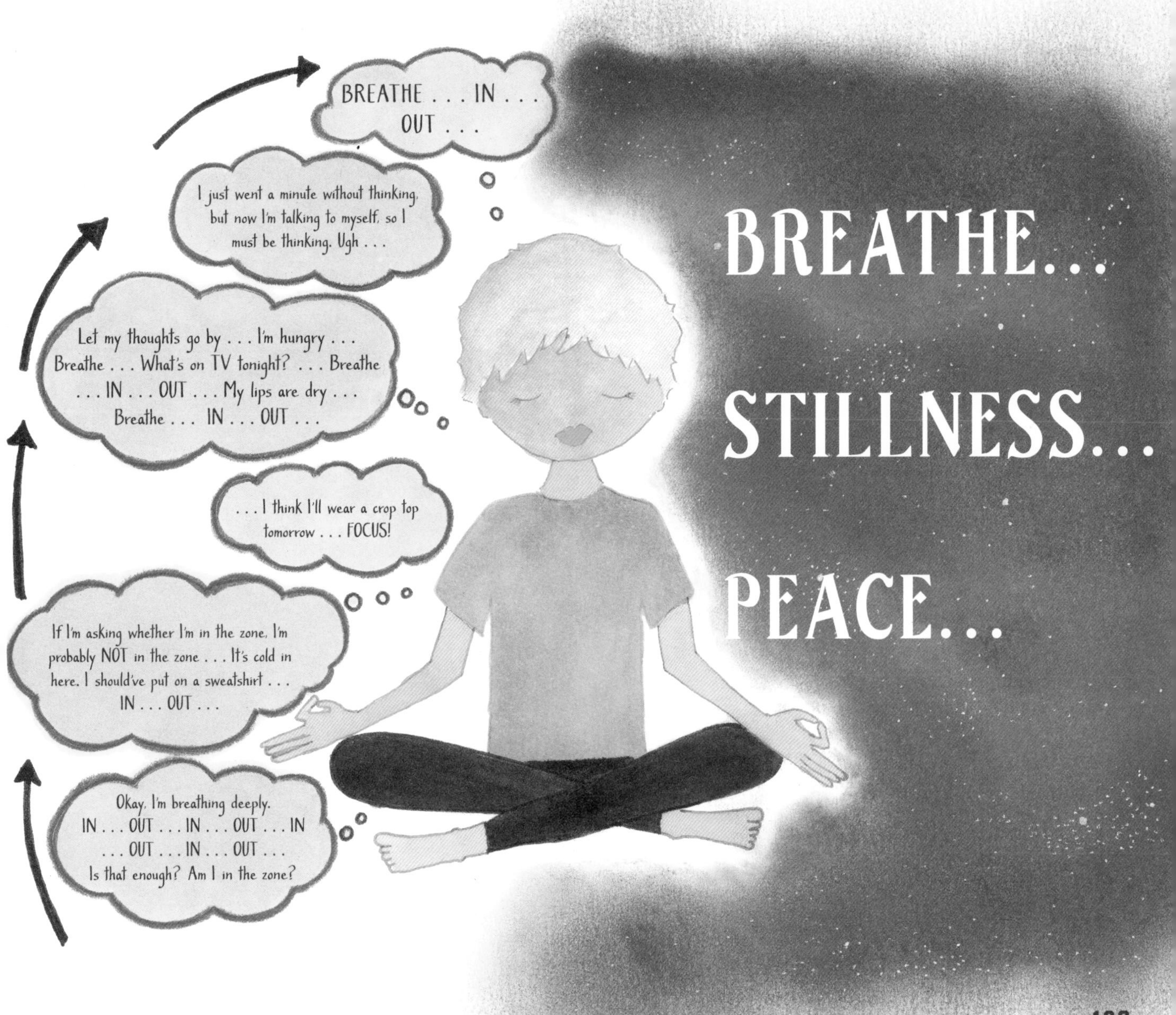

ENERGY & VIBES: THE INVISIBLE FIELD

You're beginning to get the picture, right? You're waking up to the unseen powers within and around you, powers you didn't know you had. One of those unseen powers is energy, but let's call it your vibe, which is short for vibration.

When you walk into a room, your vibe surrounds you. Every mood you have, whether it's happy, angry, sad, or scared, holds a certain energy that cannot be seen but certainly can be felt. Think about how you feel when someone who is angry comes into the room. They don't even have to speak a word, and instantly you can feel the vibe of anger. When someone joyful enters a room, it's like sunshine just walked in. Do you know anyone whose vibe feels like pure sunshine?

Each one of us is responsible for the energy we embody and bring to others. The vibration of our bodies can help us attract positive experiences. If you want other people to meet you with good energy, you have to become mindful of what vibe you are bringing into the room so you can be met with that positive energy. When you make a conscious choice to enter a room and carry yourself in a joyful vibration, you have a better chance of being met by a similar energy.

INVISIBLE FIELD

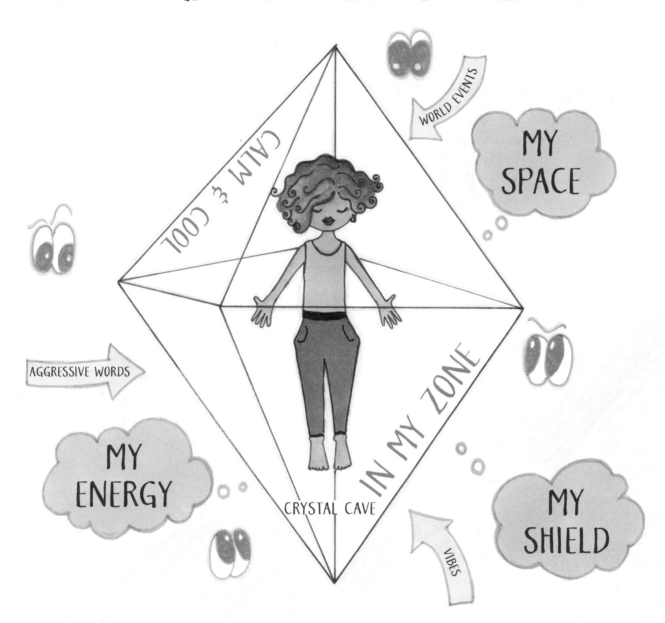

Because our invisible fields broadcast our feelings on an energetic level to the outside world, we can sometimes tune in to other people's fields and energies without trying. While it's wonderful to be an empathic person and be compassionate to others, sometimes we can absorb other people's heavy or negative energies. Moods are contagious.

To prevent this, School of Awake recommends making a conscious decision to focus on your own invisible field to help shift your energy to a heart-centered, uplifted vibe. In that space, your invisible field is not only giving out good energy to others but is also attracting good energy. How can you do this? By being mindful of what you are thinking, and making a conscious choice to be positive and present.

Sometimes, though, we need to cleanse the energies we absorb so we can feel like our joyful selves again. To do this, we use a technique called *cleansing our invisible field*. The best way to do this is to visualize a shape like 2 pyramids stacked, wide base to wide base, which you can think of as your crystal cave.

HOW TO USE YOUR INVISIBLE FIELD

Take some time to become quiet, close your eyes, and focus by picturing yourself inside your crystal cave. It protects your invisible field, and you can make it as big or small as you like in your mind's eye. It's fun to play with the size. It can be as big as a house, or it can hug you tight. Give it a try right now. Here are some other ways to experiment:

- Fill your crystal cave with positive energy by thinking positive thoughts or repeating an affirmation. This will shield you from any harsh energies or heavy vibes from others.

- Fill your crystal cave with a color chosen from the School of Awake color chart (on page 119) to enhance your invisible field.

- Before you walk into a room, surround yourself with your crystal cave if you anticipate feeling sensitive or needing some extra good energy.

PROTECTIVE LAYERS: HOODIES

Have you ever been in a mood where all you wanted to wear was a hooded sweatshirt? School of Awake considers hoodies the staple piece of any wardrobe. Even though we don't believe in uniforms, hoodies are the one item that is a must. We LOVE hoodies because they feel so cozy and so right.

Hoodies have been around for centuries in many cultures. Monks are spiritual students who study the art of quietness and oneness, and in many traditions monks wear hooded robes (hoodies!) to stay quiet and block out distraction. Hooded robes provide them with extra privacy and personal space. They can pull up their hood and block out the world. Hoodies have evolved into universal fashion must-haves. Plus, they look good on everybody!

When we wear hoodies, our ears and heads are covered. That feels safe, as if we're enclosed in a personal cocoon, and some days we just need to block out the noise of the world. The hoodie can enclose your energy field when you feel extra sensitive — and it keeps you warm when you're chilly, too! Hoodies are like wearable hugs.

OUT OF THIS WORLD

- There is joy in this world, and there is sadness in this world. Everything in life has an opposite.

- Sometimes you will feel like you want to escape. Sometimes you will wish you could be somewhere else that does not have the pressures and pain that this world has, and that's normal. But before you choose to escape through zoning out on your phone or device, snacking away on sugar, or sitting in front of the TV, try to sit with the discomfort and try to dissolve it by visually creating a place you design that only you have access to.

- You'd be amazed at how much power your imagination can have on the neurotransmitters of your brain. Science has proved that when we visualize a happy moment, the neurons in the brain respond by relaying that happy message throughout the body. We can shift our mood powerfully with the techniques we've learned at School of Awake!

- Use your vivid imagination to create the perfect place, a universe you can visit whenever you want, where everything is just the way you want it. Create your own perfect virtual escape. School of Awake believes in the power of the imagination and creating our own custom safe places that can comfort us. Psychotherapists have used this technique and proved that these mental vacations, even for just a few minutes, can bring us back to a feeling of calm.

"The future belongs to those who believe in the beauty of their dreams."
—ELEANOR ROOSEVELT

ACTIVITY ⚠ ALERT

YOUNIVERSE

CREATE A VIRTUAL ESCAPE!

Just for ME!

SUPPLIES

- Piece of plain white paper
- Colored pencils, markers, or crayons
- YOUR IMAGINATION

There are no limits to Youniverse.

OUT OF THIS WORLD

Use your creative imagination to create the perfect place, a universe you can visit whenever you want, where everything is just the way you want it. Draw your safe place, your own virtual escape. Add your Youniverse drawing to your S.O.A. tool kit.

Escape

Create

Dream

Imagine

A CLASS ACT: MANNERS & ETIQUETTE

SCHOOL OF AWAKE

TRUST IN THE UNIVERSE WE

EST 2017

CHAPTER NINE

Manners are the way we do things and how we present ourselves to the world. Manners are what we leave behind as our signature when we leave a room. They are how we are remembered. There is a certain dignity in respecting our environment and other people, and having nice manners conveys to the world how we feel about ourselves inside. When we are mindful, manners come much more easily.

Etiquette is how we put our manners to use in our physical environment. When you meet someone who says "please" and "thank you" and eats nicely, is courteous to others, and makes eye contact while talking, have you noticed that you automatically think, "Wow, this person really stands out"? When we are rushing or not aware of how we are moving through our days, it's easy to have bad etiquette. Sloppy eating, open-mouth chewing, interrupting people, throwing around insults and criticisms about people or places — this is bad etiquette, and it's not cute. All it takes is a good amount of practice and presence to learn good etiquette. Having good etiquette generates self-respect and helps us build even more confidence. Carrying ourselves with grace is a natural by-product of self-love.

If you stay mindful about your manners and how you carry yourself in the world, before you know it, you will be turning heads with your classy sass.

Are You a Queen?

What comes to mind when you think of a queen? Do you think about how people around her respect her? Queens have beautiful manners. Queens carry themselves with respect and grace, poise and presence. We are all potential queens, and working on our manners and etiquette puts us on our throne and brings us the respect we deserve.

Rank how true each statement is for you on a scale of 1 to 5, with 1 meaning it's never true and 5 meaning it's always true.

MANNERS QUIZ

	1	2	3	4	5
When I walk into a room, I walk with confidence.					
I make eye contact when I listen and speak to others.					
I do kind things for others, even if no one is watching.					
I say "please" and "thank you."					
I chew with my mouth closed.					

135

	1	2	3	4	5
I say "sorry" when I have hurt someone.					
I wash my hands before I eat.					
I only put as much food on my plate as I can eat.					
I feel that it's unkind to leave cruel or critical comments on other people's social media.					
When I cough or sneeze, I cover my mouth.					
I wash my hands after using the restroom.					
When I make a mess, I clean it up.					
I am respectful of my elders.					
I am aware and respectful of other people's personal space.					
I respect other people's things, and I ask permission before I touch or borrow them.					
If I open something, I close it afterward.					
I hold the door open for others.					
When I'm not feeling well, I stay home or keep my distance from people so I won't get anyone else sick.					
When I burp, I cover my mouth and say "excuse me."					
I take good care of my body and keep myself clean and looking my best.					
I keep my space neat and organized.					
I listen without interrupting.					
I put my napkin in my lap when I am eating.					
I help my friends and family when they are having a hard time.					
I am aware of my noise level when I am around others.					
I treat others the way I want to be treated.					
I give away the things I no longer need so that someone else may use them.					
When I see trash, I pick it up.					
I am original with my creativity. I try not to copy other people's style or ideas.					
When someone asks how I am doing, I tell them and then politely ask how they are doing as well.					

Your Royal Score

30 – 60 POINTS:

You are a Dame, in the Queen's Court, but have some work left to do. Get to it!

60 – 80 POINTS:

You are a Countess, on your way, but there's more to learn. Practice makes perfect!

80 – 100 POINTS:

You are a Duchess, not too shabby, but there's still room for improvement. Keep up the good work!

100 – 140 POINTS:

You are a Grand Princess. You know quite a lot about manners.
With just a little more effort, you'll be a Queen!

140 – 160 POINTS:

You are a Queen, the epitome of manners and grace!
Congratulations, Your Majesty!

THE ETERNAL JEWELS: VIRTUES

CHAPTER TEN

At School of Awake, we study and embody eternal jewels called virtues. Virtues are our positive character traits rooted in our basic goodness as human beings and our universal connection to one another. Virtues are the source of the small, kind deeds we do for others that uplift our day as well as theirs. Virtues, such as compassion and integrity, go beyond words and culture and get to the heart of our humanity, the core of our stardust nature, the thing that connects us all.

Some virtues we are born with, almost like gifts, or they develop naturally. Others we have to intentionally practice over and over to make them strong, to make them into the indestructible jewels that they can be. Virtues are more precious than any material thing. They are indestructible and we keep them forever. But virtues are meaningless without actions. These treasures must be honored, and we should use them to guide our daily lives.

School of Awake suggests you pick one virtue each day to polish and admire. Use it throughout the day to experience what it means and to share it with other people. Read on for a description of the most important virtues.

Virtues can shine light throughout the mini universe that is you, and they are also gifts you can share with others.

Today I will practice...(pick your virtue).

PASSION Unstoppable enthusiasm Find it . . .	**WISDOM** Your inner knowing Learn it . . .	**ACCEPTANCE** Letting things be what they are Welcome it . . .	**RESILIENCE** The ability to keep your head up Do it . . .	**KINDNESS** Niceness from your heart Give it . . .
ACCOUNTABILITY Being responsible for your actions Recognize it . . .	**HUMILITY** Knowing not to brag, even when you can Practice it . . .	**CONFIDENCE** Letting your soul glow Own it . . .	**FAITH** Believing in what's to come Trust it . . .	**PRESENCE** Living in the moment Discover it . . .
GENEROSITY Spirit of giving Share it . . .	**CONSIDERATION** Thinking about others' feelings Embody it . . .	**S.O.A.** ♥ **VIRTUES**	**RESPECT** Treating yourself and others with high regard Have it . . .	**GRATITUDE** Being thankful Treasure it . . .
INTEGRITY Being honest in all you do Carry it . . .	**OPTIMISM** Seeing the glass as half full Pursue it . . .	**CURIOSITY** The desire to learn about anything Explore it . . .	**BRAVERY** Having courage in the face of darkness Honor it . . .	**COMPASSION** Feeling someone else's pain Notice it . . .
JOY Being your happy self Follow it . . .	**AUTHENTICITY** Keeping it real Live it . . .	**HUMOR** Nothing is better than laughing Enjoy it . . .	**FORGIVENESS** Letting it go Know it . . .	**CONNECTION** Uniting as one Seek it . . .

OPTIMISM: Optimism means being hopeful about the future, being cheerful, looking for the good, and keeping the attitude that things will work out for the best even when situations are looking down. Optimism creates resilience, and it gives us the flexibility to find solutions and recover quickly during difficult circumstances. It feels like having hope, seeing the glass half full instead of half empty. When we are optimistic, we feel happy and leave room for grace.

S.O.A. SUPERNOVA

An outstanding example of optimism and resilience, HELEN KELLER was born in 1880, and when she was 19 months old suffered an illness that left her deaf and blind. Exceedingly bright, she studied her surroundings through touch, smell, and taste. Keller struggled for years to learn to speak so that others would understand her. She eventually attended Radcliffe College and went on to advocate for women's right to vote, pacifism, and birth control. In 1920 she helped found the American Civil Liberties Union.

COMPASSION: Compassion is imagining yourself in the place of someone else, as though you could swap minds and bodies with that person and feel how it feels to become them. Compassion links us to our tenderness and opens our hearts big enough to understand an experience besides our own. Compassion taps into our sensitive sides to give us a feeling of caring for another person's situation. Being compassionate makes us more tolerant. Without compassion we are critics and perfectionists with not much room for learning and growing. When you see someone suffering on any level, try to feel compassion for that person. It will inspire you to be helpful toward someone in any way you can be.

"The most beautiful people we have known are those who have known defeat, known suffering, known struggle, known loss, and have found their way out of the depths. These persons have an appreciation, a sensitivity, and an understanding of life that fills them with compassion, gentleness, and a deep loving concern. Beautiful people do not just happen."

—ELISABETH KÜBLER-ROSS

"Be kind, for everyone you meet is fighting a hard battle."

—IAN MACLAREN

HUMOR: At School of Awake, we love to laugh. Finding humor in even the most difficult situations can bring relief and lightheartedness. If we don't have laughter or a sense of humor in this crazy game called life, things can get way too serious, and fast! Life needs space for comedy. Sometimes things go wrong as if they'd been perfectly orchestrated to go wrong. Sometimes, the universe has a wicked sense of humor, and we have to try to find the funny in the not-so-funny because laughing lightens the load. There is always something funny to laugh at, even if it's yourself now and then. What feels better than laughing? Next time you start to take yourself or a situation too seriously, try to find something funny about the situation. Laughter is medicine for the soul. Nothing feels better than a good old laugh.

FACT Laughter makes you feel good mentally and physically, and it's good for you. It is like mental jogging because it increases your heart rate and afterward your muscles relax. Laughing relieves stress and boosts our immune system.

"I love people who make me laugh. I honestly think it's the thing I like most, to laugh. It cures a multitude of ills. It's probably the most important thing in a person."

—AUDREY HEPBURN

> *"The more you praise and celebrate your life, the more there is in life to celebrate."*
> —OPRAH WINFREY

GRATITUDE:

Gratitude is your heart's full expression of thankfulness and contentment. There is always something to be grateful for. School of Awake likes to practice the attitude of gratitude for all that life gives us. The list of things to be grateful for is so long! We can start with the shelter we have, the friendships we cherish, the food we eat, sunlight warming the earth every day. Every day when you open your eyes, you are receiving a gift of life and light, and by being thankful for small and large blessings, we polish this jewel. Beautiful experiences blossom when they are appreciated. When we shift our focus from the things we don't have to the gifts we do have, we begin to see how full our lives truly are. Gratitude helps us cultivate compassion for other people in the world. From the clean air we breathe to the shoes on our feet, there is always someone who has less than we do. Being of service to other beings helps increase our own awareness of the good in our lives. With gratitude and service, we feel fulfilled and are not constantly wanting more or something new. We look around and feel thankful for all of life. Thank you. Thank you. Thank you!

HUMILITY:

Being humble means doing great things without needing to be praised or recognized. Humble people remain open to learning more and becoming better without receiving attention. Being humble means being down-to-earth and being yourself with no walls up. It means knowing you are not better than anyone else. By letting go of a certain, expected result and simply letting your actions and talents speak for themselves, no recognition or reward expected, you ditch your ego.

A humble artist paints an amazing painting and does not announce how beautiful the painting is. Instead, she simply makes room for something beautiful to move through her and allows that beauty to touch others through her art. Her sense of self-worth is not dependent on someone else's praise of the beautiful painting. This is where true self-esteem comes from. We do not own our talents and gifts. We are vessels that open up to the spirit of creativity and make space for greatness to work through us. Humility reminds us that at an essential level we are all the same, all made from stardust.

> *"True humility is not thinking less of yourself; it is thinking of yourself less."*
> —C. S. LEWIS

SNACK ALERT
Dab & Dip Gratitude Delight

Sometimes the simplest things are the best!
Even better when shared with friends!

DAB CUCUMBERS!

DIP CHIPS!

DIP PITA BREAD!

DAB CARROTS!

DAB CELERY!

DIP BROCCOLI!

DAB PEPPERS!

DIP PRETZELS!

INGREDIENTS

- One 8-ounce can garbanzo beans, drained
- 4 ounces white beans (half of an 8-ounce can), drained
- 1 clove garlic, crushed
- Juice of 1 lemon
- $1/4$ to $1/2$ teaspoon ground cumin
- 2 teaspoons olive oil
- Salt & pepper

DIRECTIONS

Blend all ingredients except salt & pepper in the blender until smooth. Add salt & pepper to taste.

FROM THE SCHOOL OF AWAKE KITCHEN

CONFIDENCE: Confidence is loving and believing in who we are with no apologies. Confidence makes us feel good about our lives and the things that we do and accomplish. Confidence feels like being who we are and not hiding anything about ourselves. We are our own biggest cheerleaders, and we can build our confidence by taking the time out to compliment ourselves when we do great on something. Being a good person builds confidence. Being true to ourselves and our HeartStar also builds healthy confidence. Confidence is knowing our self-worth and carrying ourselves with respect. Knowing who we are and not comparing ourselves to others also builds our confidence. This self-love starts to add up inside, and before we know it, we are confident! We love ourselves, and we are not scared or shy to share who we are or the talents we are blessed with.

There is a difference between being overconfident and being self-confident. Self-confidence is humble and is inclusive of other people. Overconfidence is being inflated like a balloon and thinking we're better than everyone else. It's a fine line. Staying aware of others helps us be confident but not overconfident.

GENEROSITY: Being generous means being giving with our resources. It means being open to share whatever we have — and not just sharing things, but also sharing ourselves and our spirit with others. We are giving of the best parts of ourselves to the people around us. Being generous softens us and reminds us we are connected to other people and to all living things.

Give generously of your talents and whatever else you have, including knowledge, time, and material items such as clothing. Provide help to others. We all need each other. Look how nature provides for the needs of plants and all living beings, and use that as your inspiration to give — and give as much as you can! When we are generous, we expand and open to allow abundance to flow back to ourselves, like a flower opening to receive the gifts of the sun.

FAITH: Faith is a beautiful word that's often used in religions to describe believing in a higher power. Faith means trusting life and walking with that trust through daily events, knowing that all is well. Faith is having complete confidence that circumstances and outcomes will work out for the best.

Living in a faithful way is a journey, not just a destination. Exercising our trust in faith includes the times when we are at our lowest points and feel like giving up. Faith means still believing even when we can't see any signs of a positive outcome. This is when faith is most important. Whatever our religious or spiritual beliefs are, living with faith allows grace into our lives and leaves room for the unexpected goodness to open up in our worlds. School of Awake believes in leaving space for magic to come through. We continue to believe that all is well, all is in divine order, and a higher source is ultimately loving us and guiding us. It's a simple attitude of positivity that comes from within ourselves. We are believers at School of Awake.

S.O.A. SUPERNOVA

HARRIET TUBMAN lived from 1822 to 1913. She was born as a slave but believed that she could be free. After a horrific injury caused by a white man who had hit her with a lead weight, Harriet began seeing things and falling asleep uncontrollably. Yet she used her dreams and her faith to create maps to freedom for many other people, risking her own life to guide hundreds of slaves to freedom on the Underground Railroad. As she described it, she could "fly like a bird" over landscapes, mapping out the safest routes to freedom. Now that's vision and faith!

INTEGRITY: Integrity means thinking and acting from a place of honesty, and it's an important virtue to cultivate in this time. People with integrity are trustworthy because they hold their values and principles close to their heart, and everything they do comes from acting from their highest selves for the greater good of everyone around.

To develop integrity you have to have high standards for your own beliefs and values, and you have to act in accordance with those beliefs and values. Integrity will spill over into every part of your life for the best. With integrity, you can become a good example to others and be a trusted leader. People who possess integrity have respect for themselves and the outcome of their actions. Integrity requires you to think before you act, rather than having a knee-jerk reaction. The people we admire who do good things for others and the world have integrity because they are connected with the goodness inside their hearts and they take pride in the choices they make. In simpler terms: do the right thing.

"The weak can never forgive.
Forgiveness is the attribute
of the strong."

—MAHATMA GANDHI

FORGIVENESS: One of the most difficult but also one of the most rewarding virtues is forgiveness. People are going to make mistakes, including you. That's part of life. And sometimes people purposely harm you. When you choose not to forgive, you carry around the burden of sadness, anger, and grief in your body. Notice how you feel when you think of someone who has done something completely unforgivable. Your whole body tenses up, anger rises, and sadness or grief takes control. Forgiveness frees you from being stuck in these feelings. Sometimes our inability to forgive stems from our own pain, and even a tiny gesture toward forgiveness will help. Forgiveness is not to be confused with weakness. It's the opposite. Being able to forgive is true strength because you are making a choice not to poison yourself with negativity. You choose not to carry this burden in your body. Forgiveness is also filled with compassion for our own shortcomings and others' as well. Drop the negativity like bad trash. Shake it off. We learn to forgive for our own benefit. Think of forgiveness as a gift to yourself.

Large doses of forgiveness and gratitude can bring you through almost anything.

LOVE: Last but certainly not least is the virtue of love. Love is the greatest gift we can receive and give in this lifetime. There are so many ways to experience love. We feel love for our families, animals, our friends, and our crushes, and sometimes even when we just see a beautiful sunset or view. Love lives inside us, and love also lives in giving to others. Helping someone who is in need, being kind to people, and extending ourselves all come from the love we have inside. We are built of love. Some of us have a harder time accessing it than others, but it's still there. Even saying the word *love* feels good.

"The best and most beautiful things in the world cannot be seen nor even touched, but just felt in the heart."

—HELEN KELLER

S.O.A. MOMENT

- Pick 1 virtue from the list and practice applying it to yourself.

- Whenever you feel you are limited or stuck, dip into your virtue jewel box (see next page), pick a jewel, and watch it shine and brighten the situation.

S.O.A. TOOL KIT

ACTIVITY ⚠ ALERT
Virtue ◇ Jewels

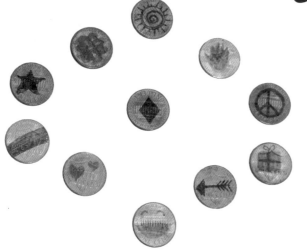

SUPPLIES

- 11 pennies
- 1 or more colored permanent markers

DRAW THESE VIRTUE ICONS ON YOUR PENNIES:

JOY	COMPASSION	HUMOR	GRATITUDE	KINDNESS	HUMILITY
SUNSHINE	HEARTS	SMILEY FACE	FLOWER	HEART IN HAND	ARROW

CONFIDENCE	GENEROSITY	INTEGRITY	FAITH	FORGIVENESS
STAR	PRESENT	DIAMOND	RAINBOW	PEACE SIGN

VIRTUE JEWEL BOX

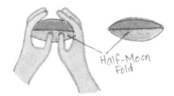

When you're done, put your jewel box in your tool kit!

SUPPLIES

- 1 cardboard toilet paper roll
- 1 or more acrylic paints
- 1 or more permanent markers for decorating
- Your 11 virtue jewels

Step 1

Open the toilet paper roll into a rectangle shape.

Step 2

Half-Moon Fold

Fold the end of one side in toward the center. It should make a crease that looks like a half-moon shape.

Step 3

side view

Fold in the other side to make another half moon. The ends should overlap slightly.

Step 4

side view

Repeat steps 2 and 3 on the other end of the roll.

Step 5

Open the roll and paint it any color you want. Let it dry.

Step 6

Fold it back into a box and decorate it. Add little designs, inspiring words, whatever your HeartStar desires . . .

Step 7

Open one end and put your virtue jewels inside for safe keeping.

Step 8

Close your eyes, shake your box, and pick out one of your jewels. Honor that virtue throughout the day.

SO YOU'RE TELLING ME THIS BECAUSE...?

Having a strong sense of values and knowing how and when to apply a virtue to a life experience is one of the greatest assets you can build. Virtues are dependent upon your willingness to develop them, much like muscles that respond to exercise. The more you use them, the more you'll see their value and how powerful they can be. These jewels are perfect tools not only for overcoming obstacles but also for growing and expanding beyond what you think you are capable of.

We each have a responsibility to become the best version of ourselves, and that means we have to honestly look at who we are and how we operate in our lives. It's always good to hold a mirror to ourselves and question our reaction to a situation before we blame someone else.

Virtues are like a circle of friends that all hold hands. Once you get to know one really well, you automatically welcome the next one. Without courage, how could you know forgiveness? Without integrity, how could you know respect? Generosity introduces us to kindness. Authenticity is right next to bravery. All the virtues intertwine with each other.

Using your virtues will make you feel really good inside, and the inner beauty that you develop through polishing these jewels will last your whole life. Virtues are a gift to yourself and this world. Polish your eternal jewels daily. Be beautiful inside.

LOVE

Amor (ah-moor) — Spanish

αγάπη (ah-ga-pee) — Greek

Kärlek (shaw-leck) — Swedish

愛 (eye) — Chinese

Liebe (lee-buh) — German

люблю (lyu-blyu) — Russian

אהבה (ah-hah-vah) — Hebrew

愛 (ai) — Japanese

Amour (ah-moor) — French

Upendo (oo-pend-o) — Swahili

حـب (hubb) — Arabic

Aşk (ashk) — Turkish

मोहब्बत (mo-hab-bat) — Hindi

Grá (graw) — Gaelic

사랑 (sarang) — Korean

Amore (ah-more-ay) — Italian

"Love is the bridge between you and everything." —RUMI

SCHOOL OF AWAKE
CREST JEWEL STUDENT CONTRACT

We follow our inner voices & trust our hearts.

We consider how our actions affect other people.

We breathe and become mindful before we speak.

We honor nature and all living creatures.

We forgive.

We make decisions from a place of self-love.

We stay positive & believe in dreams coming true.

We do not give away our power.

We treat our bodies like temples.

We give selfless service to those in need.

We walk in gratitude.

We take responsibility for our own lives.

CLOSING

Our lives are precious. Every second that we are breathing and living, we are contributing to this world and everything we are connected to. This is why it is so important to become our best selves and operate from love so that our contribution to this world is a positive one.

What we want to leave you with is this: Don't ever forget how lovable you are and that you are a sparkling, shimmering star in this beautiful galaxy. You are a one-of-a-kind creation that has come to shine your unique light in this universe. Believe in yourself. Stay true to yourself. Love yourself. Be loving to other people. Every possibility you can dream of begins with you! No matter what happens in this life, invite your HeartStar to lead you, and you will always be the supreme you. Use your tools and stay awake!

Love,

Kidada

ACKNOWLEDGMENTS

To my parents, who are also my dearest friends: Thank you for all you have given me. I am profoundly grateful. I adore you both deeply.

Thank you to my S.O.A. team, Nikole Magana, Koa Jones, Erin Sermeus, Georgia Hughes, Tracy Cunningham, and New World Library: Thank you for your loyal, loving support, your enthusiasm, and your grounded energy that gave this project the structure it needed! I'm so grateful. I love you guys.

To my family and close friends: I love you. Thank you for everything. Your friendship and support mean so much to me.

To Rashida: Thank you for setting up the first lunch that changed everything. I love you.

Mommy: My love for you knows no limits.

Dr. G! Your patience is profound. Love you.

To Kathy and Jeff Cannon: Thank you for everything.

James Adams and Seth Horwitz: Thank you for your expertise.

Penny, you are my forever love.

Regina, you always have the right words. I love you.

To all the powerful women throughout history who have paved the way for me to find my voice: I cherish your bravery and strength. Thank you.

Last but not least, to God and my Ancestors, Guides, Angels, and dear beloved ones on the other side: Thank you for your constant guidance, wisdom, and love. I feel your presence in my life every day. We are together forever.

ABOUT KIDADA JONES

Kidada Jones has worked as a model, fashion designer, stylist, and brand consultant. Kidada found her unique style at a young age, mixing the whimsical and contemporary to create her trademark aesthetic. Through it all, she has remained a spiritual seeker, and this book is the culmination of her journeys, presenting deep wisdom through an inviting, open combination of words and art. Kidada lives in California.

ABOUT KOA JONES

A childhood friend of Kidada's, Koa Jones grew up in Southern California, with art in her heart and an affinity for drawing, painting, and creating arts and crafts. Koa has worked as an art teacher for children and as a freelance artist. As a young girl, she struggled with shyness and finding her voice, so when Kidada asked her to be a part of this incredible book, Koa jumped at the chance. She lives with her two children, Renzo and Linnea, in Woodland Hills, California.

ABOUT NIKOLE MAGANA

Nikole Magana has served as a brand manager and graphic designer with Kidada Jones since 2008. She has done in-house and freelance brand development and graphic design for many well-known companies. She is a certified Ayurvedic Panchakarma Therapist and has two Chihuahua mixes, Frijolito and Gigi Rose, whom she loves dearly!

NEW WORLD LIBRARY

14 Pamaron Way • Novato • California • 94949

www.newworldlibrary.com

School of Awake, HeartStar, and G.I.F.T. are trademarks of Lakshmi Deluxe, Inc.

Text design and typesetting by *theBookDesigners*

LIBRARY OF CONGRESS CATALOGING-IN-PUBLICATION DATA

NAMES: Jones, Kidada, [date]–, author. | Jones, Koa, illustrator.

TITLE: School of awake : a girl's guide to the universe / Kidada Jones, illustrations by Koa Jones.

DESCRIPTION: Novato, California: New World Library, [2017]

IDENTIFIERS: LCCN 2017013726 (print) | LCCN 2017030964 (ebook)

| ISBN 9781608684595 (Ebook) | ISBN 9781608684588 (alk. paper)

SUBJECTS: LCSH: Girls — Psychology — Juvenile literature. | Teenage girls — Psychology — Juvenile literature.

| Self-realization — Juvenile literature. | Spiritual life–Juvenile literature.

CLASSIFICATION: LCC HQ798 (ebook) | LCC HQ798 .J665 2017 (print) | DDC 155.43/3–dc23

LC record available at https://lccn.loc.gov/2017013726

First printing, October 2017

ISBN 978-1-60868-458-8

Ebook ISBN 978-1-60868-459-5

Printed in Canada on 30% postconsumer-waste recycled paper

 New World Library is proud to be a Gold Certified Environmentally Responsible Publisher.

Publisher certification awarded by Green Press Initiative. www.greenpressinitiative.org

10 9 8 7 6 5 4 3 2 1

NEW WORLD LIBRARY is dedicated to publishing books and other media that inspire and challenge us to improve the quality of our lives and the world.

We are a socially and environmentally aware company. We recognize that we have an ethical responsibility to our customers, our staff members, and our planet.

We serve our customers by creating the finest publications possible on personal growth, creativity, spirituality, wellness, and other areas of emerging importance. We serve New World Library employees with generous benefits, significant profit sharing, and constant encouragement to pursue their most expansive dreams.

As a member of the Green Press Initiative, we print an increasing number of books with soy-based ink on 100 percent postconsumer-waste recycled paper. Also, we power our offices with solar energy and contribute to nonprofit organizations working to make the world a better place for us all. Our products are available in bookstores everywhere.

LET'S CONNECT

www.newworldlibrary.com

At NewWorldLibrary.com you can download our catalog, subscribe to our e-newsletter, read our blog, and link to authors' websites, videos, and podcasts.

Find us on Facebook, follow us on Twitter, watch us on YouTube, and listen to the *New World Now* podcast.

Send your questions and comments our way! You make it possible for us to do what we love to do.

Phone: 415-884-2100 or 800-972-6657
Catalog requests: Ext. 10 | **Orders:** Ext. 10 | **Fax:** 415-884-2199
escort@newworldlibrary.com

NEW WORLD LIBRARY
publishing books that change lives
14 Pamaron Way, Novato, CA 94949